The
HAPPINESS
FORMULA

$$\frac{\text{HOPE}}{\text{HUNGER}} = \text{HAPPINESS}$$

A Scientific, Groundbreaking Approach to Happiness and Personal Fulfillment

Alphonsus Obayuwana, MD, PhD, CPC

Health Communi⟨
Boca Raton, ⟨

www.hcibooks.com

T0017789

The PISA Scale is copyrighted. No one may use it for any reason without the written permission of the Triple-H Project, LLC., P.O. Box 45, Perrysburg, OH 43551, USA. Or go to *www.triplehproject.com* for alternative contact information. The reader's purchase of this book automatically constitutes permission to use the PISA Scale for personal self-assessment, but all other uses or users are prohibited. Every publication resulting from the use of the PISA Scale requires attribution or acknowledgment of the author.

Library of Congress Cataloging-in-Publication Data
is available through the Library of Congress

© 2024 Alphonsus Obayuwana, MD, PhD, CPC

ISBN-13: 978-07573-2508-3 (Paperback)
ISBN-10: 07573-2508-4 (Paperback)
ISBN-13: 978-07573-2509-0 (ePub)
ISBN-10: 07573-2509-2 (ePub)

Publisher: Health Communications, Inc.
　　　　301 Crawford Boulevard, Suite 200
　　　　Boca Raton, FL 33432-3762

Cover, interior design and formatting by Larissa Hise Henoch.
Author photo by Michele Kipplen Photography.

CONTENTS

ACKNOWLEDGMENTS

I t took me over three decades to amass enough information to
make the concept of this book reasonable. Along the way, I had
assistance from so many people that it is impossible to acknowledge, by name, all those who contributed in one way or another. I
have therefore decided to recognize institutions and categories of
people rather than express my thanks to each one of my countless
individual contributors.

First, I want to recognize and express my gratitude to key institutions that made those incremental contributions that ultimately
made the very concept of this book plausible: Howard University
College of Medicine, University of Maryland College of Medicine,
the Johns Hopkins School of Medicine, Eastern Virginia Medical
School, and Ohio University College of Osteopathic Medicine, in
Athens—including the Smith-Kline Medical Perspective Fellowship
and its research grant that started it all.

Next, my acknowledgement goes to the five major hospitals or
medical centers where most of my work was done: Harbor Hospital Center, Baltimore; Francis Scott Key Medical Center, Glen

Burnie; Shady Grove Adventist Hospital, Bethesda; Maryview Medical Center, Portsmouth; and St. Vincent Medical Center, Toledo, Ohio, for their scholarly environment, competent staff, and excellent resources.

My most profound gratitude goes to those hundreds of medical students, nursing students, nurses, nursing supervisors, resident physicians, medical fellows, and attending physician colleagues who answered multiple surveys, volunteered as subjects, participated as controls, went on international medical missions with me, and helped collate data both inside and outside the US. Particularly, I owe a special debt of gratitude to Mark Malatesta, my irreplaceable consultant and adviser; friends and longtime collaborators, like Drs. James Collins, Robert Barnett Jr., Georgia Dustin, John Allotey, Ramu Perni, John Sampson, and Osaretin Idusuyi, for their invaluable support.

To my family: my dear wife Ann; our sons, Asiri and Iyare; our daughters, Bertha and Judith; granddaughters, Uki, Ivie, and Enibokun, I say thank you for your patience and willingness to give me both space and time for research and writing.

Finally, my sincerest gratitude goes to my very responsive literary agent, Steven Harris, my incredibly resourceful editor, Christine Belleris, my irresistible publicist, Lindsey Triebel, Larissa Henoch, for designing the cover and inside of the book so beautifully, and Health Communications, Inc., the Life Issues Publisher, for believing in me and making it possible to bring *The Happiness Formula* manuscript to light as a book.

WHY THIS BOOK?

I wrote this book for four major reasons:
1. To share my chance discovery of a simple equation that makes it possible, for the first time ever, to measure happiness both subjectively and objectively—simultaneously.
2. To introduce the Edo Questionnaire, a twelve-item self-assessment tool for differentiating flourishing individuals from languishing individuals; and in between these two extremes, also to help identify *happy, unhappy, very happy* or *very unhappy* members of a cohort—regardless of any cultural and socio-economic differences.
3. To offer a strong theoretical basis and a firm practical structure for happiness coaching as there are no existing standards to guide happiness coaches.
4. To provide happiness seekers with a proven routine for achieving and sustaining a flourishing life.

Happiness is *not* a luxury. It is a human necessity. In fact, it is existential to life itself. For happiness seekers, therefore, happiness coaches, happiness advocates, directors of human services, chief happiness officers, researchers, and policymakers involved directly or indirectly in the "business" of human happiness, this book is for you—as no one can effectively improve what one cannot accurately measure.

INTRODUCTION

Happiness is the meaning and purpose of life,
the whole aim and end of human existence.

~Aristotle

I f it is indeed true that "happiness is the meaning and purpose of life," we should all be interested in happiness. Regardless, whether aware of it or not, each of us is indeed a *happiness seeker* looking for a happier life, a *happiness advocate* assisting others to find happier lives, or a bit of both. *The Happiness Formula* will help you play either or both roles more successfully.

This book grew out of a national research grant that I was awarded to develop an instrument for measuring human hope. The Hope Index Scale (HIS) which resulted from that grant became very popular with Fortune 500 companies like Coca-Cola and General Motors, government agencies such as the Veterans Administration, and many academic institutions both inside and outside the United States.

This cutting-edge book is for readers of self-help books and those who serve in the helping professions such as life coaches, chief happiness officers, directors of human services, or other types of administrators, policy makers, and researchers who are directly or indirectly involved in the "business" of human happiness.

Unlike other books about happiness, which are too often filled with dos and don'ts, wishful thinking, and empty aphorisms, *The Happiness Formula* breaks new ground. It introduces a universal unit of measure called the Personal Happiness Index (PHI), which makes it possible—for the first time—to assign a numerical happiness score to individual humans by plugging their unique hopes, hungers, assets, and aspirations into an equation.

Happiness is very real and quite complex. It has more than one definition and many determinants. It also seems elusive because as yet there is no reliable way to measure it. Consequently, before you can convincingly and methodically increase happiness for yourself or others, you must first find a way to measure happiness so you can objectively monitor progress—or lack of progress—before and after an intervention.

As a researcher, I like to think that my work is about the "Mathematics of Happiness." That's because numbers don't lie and true mathematicians study relationships, looking for patterns and regularities to gain enough insights to make predictions about nature possible, after connecting all the dots. In the thirty-five years I have spent studying human hope and happiness, this has been my personal approach.

My interest in this area of research began when I was a medical student, working with patients admitted to the psychiatric unit because of attempted suicide. Deeply moved and transformed by these poignant encounters, I began studying human hope. When subsequently, I was awarded the national research grant and Smith-Kline Medical Perspective Fellowship to develop an instrument for measuring human hope, the purpose was to detect hopelessness early enough in troubled human individuals so assistance could be offered in time to prevent suicide. The Hope Index Scale (HIS) that I'd created, which did become very popular with well-known corporations and institutions, is at the foundation of this book.

I have served on the teaching faculty at Johns Hopkins School of Medicine, Maryland University College of Medicine, Eastern Virginia Medical School, Ohio University College of Osteopathic Medicine, and University of Toledo—teaching and mentoring thousands of medical students, resident physicians, nurses, and fellows, in the art of caring and promoting happiness for themselves and their patients. Even today, as a retired professor of medicine, I continue to teach, train, and certify happiness coaches in my current capacity as the founder and CEO of the Triple-H Project, LLC.

Despite its title, *The Happiness Formula* is much more than a mathematical equation for measuring happiness. It is a book about life, the relationship between human hope and hunger, one's overall feeling of personal satisfaction and subjective well-being.

The Happiness Formula begins by exploring *where* to look and what to look for in search of the happiest living human. This is followed by a brief history of the positive psychology movement; three happiness myths—which were all debunked; Inborn Hunger Theory, which explains why humans are in constant pursuit of happiness; and a novel mathematical formula for quantifying happiness, with detailed explanations of the variables in the equation. Finally, the book ends with major chapters on self-help and happiness coaching techniques.

To get the most out of this book, I recommend you read the chapters in the order they appear, so the intended coherent sequence of presentation and delivery is preserved. However, since this book is for happiness seekers as well as happiness advocates, the chapter summaries are presented below as an addendum to this introduction, so you can easily identify and go straight to any particularly preferred chapter of immediate interest to you.

I hope you enjoy it.

Chapter 1: The Happiest Living Human—Where to Look and What to Look For

In Chapter 1, the crowning of Finland as the happiest country in the world is challenged, since there is yet no valid universal tool for measuring happiness accurately across cultures and national boundaries. The argument is made that the current methodology for global ranking of countries is fundamentally flawed. At the end of the chapter, you will realize that no one truly yet knows the happiest country or *where* to look for the happiest living human—despite the claims in the World Happiness Report.

Chapter 2: The Dawn of Positive Psychology

In Chapter 2, a very brief history of positive psychology is presented mainly to indicate how psychologists only recently started to show interest in the subject matter of human happiness. The disease-focused psychology of the past is contrasted with the great amount of attention being paid currently to the well-being of normal everyday individuals. Examples of widening interest in the issue of human happiness in the workplace are cited with their implications for productivity, retention, innovation, and absenteeism. At the end of the chapter, you will become aware that though positive psychology has made significant strides in the study of happiness, many questions remain unanswered and there are many dots yet to be connected.

Chapter 3: Three Happiness Myths

In Chapter 3, three very popular myths about happiness are debunked. These myths claim that money cannot buy you happiness; that "happiness" means different things to different people; and happiness is too elusive to measure. At the end of this chapter, you will become aware that the contraries are true.

Chapter 4: Inborn Hunger Theory

In Chapter 4, the Inborn Hunger Theory is presented to help connect several dots in positive psychology and offer a coherent explanation as to *why, what, when, and where* human desires come from. The theory explains what makes us happy and why, what our inborn hungers do to us and for us, why young children are happier than adults, and why we all are relentlessly in pursuit of happiness. At the end of this chapter, you will know what our *five* inborn human hungers are and get a better understanding of commonly observed human behaviors that have baffled many and defied explanations.

Chapter 5: The Triple-H Equation

In Chapter 5, The Triple-H Equation, $\frac{HOPE}{HUNGER} = HAPPINESS$, which is at the core of this book, is introduced for the first time. The events leading to its deduction and the six postulates or major claims of this equation are presented. The face validity and the corroborating evidence found in the positive psychology literature are shared and discussed. Starting with *Hope*, the three variables in the equation are declared the topics of discussion in the next three subsequent chapters.

Chapter 6: Let's Talk About Hope

In Chapter 6, *Hope*, the first of the three variables in the Triple-H Equation, is deeply examined. The Chilean miners' story of survival is retold in this chapter to illustrate and affirm what hope is, where it comes from, and why we all need it. Also included and explained in this chapter is the Hope Scale with instructions on how you can measure your own level of hope. At the end of this chapter, you will know what hope is, where it comes from, why we need it, and how to measure it.

Chapter 7: The Fifteen Tenets of Human Hope

In Chapter 7, a collection of facts, impressions, conclusions, inferences, and opinions about Human Hope that I have arrived at during my decades of research are presented. Each tenet addresses a particularly important and major feature of hope by defining it, deconstructing it, explaining it, and clarifying it. Discussion of the SORKS phenomenon—a fascinating incidental finding about hope—ends the chapter.

Chapter 8: What About Hunger?

In Chapter 8, *Hunger*, the second variable in the Triple-H Equation, is defined and the five inborn human hungers (as originally observed and first documented in children) are enumerated, discussed, and explained, with multiple observable examples cited. The advantages and disadvantages of human hungers are discussed and also included in this chapter is the Hunger Scale with instructions on how you can measure your own level of hunger. At the end of this chapter, you will know what hunger is, where it comes from, what it does to us or for us, and how to measure it.

Chapter 9: That Thing We Call Happiness

In this chapter, *Happiness*, the third variable in the Triple-H Equation, is defined and its five known major triggers are presented and explained. The two types of happiness—*hedonia* and *eudaemonia*—are discussed, compared, and contrasted. The role and function of happiness in human life are explored and the primal reason for the human relentless pursuit of happiness is unveiled. The concept of Personal Happiness Index, or PHI, as a universal unit of measure of human happiness, is introduced with instructions on how you can calculate your own PHI. At the end of this chapter, you will know what happiness is, what triggers it, and how to measure it.

Chapter 10: The Big Picture

Having defined Hope, Hunger, and *Happiness* in Chapters 6, 7, and 9 respectively, Chapter 10 presents the expanded and deconstructed version of the Triple-H Equation with the three variables juxtaposed for in-depth comparison. The relationship between hope and hunger is analyzed and explained using real-life examples. What makes us happy, and why, as well as what makes us sad, and why, are explained. Also, the COVID-19 pandemic is used as a worldwide case study to illustrate how hope and hunger co-determine human happiness or unhappiness. At the end of Chapter 10, you will become aware of what makes us happy or sad and also how and why.

Chapter 11: A New Way to Measure and Quantify Happiness

In Chapter 11, the popular myth that happiness cannot be quantified is irrevocably debunked, and the PISA Scale (aka Edo Questionnaire) is presented in detail. The concept of the Personal Happiness Index (PHI) and the advantages it brings to happiness research scientists, clinicians, life coaches, chief happiness officers (CHOs), and national policy makers are explored. The Edo Questionnaire and its unique suitability as the ideal tool for global happiness surveys are presented. At the end of the chapter, you will become familiar with the administration, scoring, and interpretation of the PISA Scale and PHI—including how the happiest nation in the world can truly, scientifically, and convincingly be determined.

Chapter 12: How to Find, Keep, and Live a Happy Life

In Chapter 12, a novel definition of the term *happy life* is advanced and the five ultimate requirements for a happy life are defined, analyzed, and explained. The importance of finding your own true calling, the relevance of other people in your life, the unquestionable necessity of material resources, the power of knowledge, and the importance of spirituality in sustaining a happy life are highlighted—with clear instructions on how to boost each of these five human assets—and consequently *Hope*. At the end of Chapter 12, you will become familiar with the true definition of a happy life and will know the requirements for sustainable happiness and how to successfully find, retain, and live a happy life.

Chapter 13: Creative AIMing: A Simple Way to Find Your Life Mission

In Chapter 13, a simple method of adapting or adopting your true passion as a calling or your life mission—no matter whom you are—is fully described. At the end of this chapter, you will become aware of your own life mission or calling by simply following the instructions and suggestions provided.

Chapter 14: What to Do When Tragedy Strikes

No matter how happy one is, a personal tragedy could strike at any time. And if a tragedy does occur, how does one cope, survive, and flourish once again? In this chapter, the answers are provided. The Z Pathway and its five steps—(1) praying and spiritual uplifting, (2) counting your blessings, (3) forgiving yourself or others who have wronged you, (4) adopting a new mission (through redemptive AIMing), and (5) acceptance and moving on—are explained.

Chapter 15: Happiness Coaching: The Triple-H Method

In Chapter 15, "Happiness Coaching: The Triple-H Method," is presented to assist those coaches who may have inadequate knowledge of the science of happiness, and who therefore may be relying largely on their own intuition and personal life experiences without a strong theoretical background and well-structured practical technique in happiness coaching. At the end of the chapter, you will have a good knowledge of the art and science of happiness coaching—all based on the Triple-H Equation. Information about coaching in general is also provided.

Overview and Summary

In the overview and summary, a synopsis of *The Happiness Formula* is presented and the major impact that the Triple-H Equation can have on the ongoing human happiness dialogue is highlighted. At the end, you will have a good appreciation of the profound contribution that *The Happiness Formula* can indeed make to the human happiness chronicle.

CHAPTER 1

THE HAPPIEST LIVING HUMAN—WHERE TO LOOK AND WHAT TO LOOK FOR

Annually, since 2012, it has become customary for the United Nations to observe an International Day of Happiness. This observance occurs each year in March, and on that day the World Happiness Report is released with a global happiness ranking of all the countries around the globe. In 2023—for the sixth year in a row—*Finland* was declared the "happiest country" in the world. The ranking order for the top twenty countries was as follows:

1. Finland
2. Denmark
3. Iceland
4. Israel
5. Netherlands

6. Sweden

7. Norway

8. Switzerland

9. Luxembourg

10. New Zealand

11. Austria

12. Australia

13. Canada

14. Ireland

15. United States

16. Germany

17. Belgium

18. Czech Republic

19. United Kingdom

20. Lithuania

On the other side of the coin, Afghanistan was rated the "un-happiest country" in the world, followed by Lebanon, Sierra Leone, Zimbabwe, Congo, Botswana, Malawi, Comoros, Tanzania, Zambia, Madagascar, India, Liberia, Ethiopia, Jordan, Togo, Egypt, Mali, Gambia, and Bangladesh—in that order—for the unhappiest twenty countries.

This ranking was entirely based on Gallup World Poll surveys—during which one thousand citizens in each country were asked how satisfied they are with their lives on a scale of 0 to 10 (with 0 representing the worst possible life imaginable and 10 representing the best life possible). In 2023 specifically, the overall average score of 7.82 out of 10 by Finnish respondents is what led to the crowning of Finland as the "happiest country" in the world. Denmark got an overall average score of 7.62 out of 10 and was declared the number 2 happiest country. Iceland was declared number 3, based similarly on the overall average score of 7.56 out of 10 by one thousand citizens of Iceland. Israel was declared number 4 with an overall average score of 7.5 out of 10. Netherlands became the "fifth happiest" country because it got the average score of 7.4 out of 10.

This very simplistic, elementary, poorly informative, and hugely rudimentary method is *solely* what has been used—in the World Happiness Report to rank countries of the world—without any other considerations whatsoever. Incorrectly, it has often been implied that this ranking of nations is based on six factors—GDP, level of corruption, social support, generosity, life expectancy, and freedom of citizens—in each country. This, of course, is not true at all. The ranking has been based *solely* on the Gallup World Poll surveys— using the Cantril ladder. As already indicated above, during these surveys, respondents are simply asked how satisfied they are with their lives on a scale of 0 to10 with 0 representing the lowest rung of the ladder or the worst possible life *imaginable*; and 10 representing the best possible life *imaginable* or the highest rung of the ladder. The required *imagination* has no guide rails or boundaries to ensure some level of caution and uniformity. The respondents' ultimately chosen number on the scale of 0 to10 is heavily influenced by culture. For example, while it is not unusual in the western cultures to be boastful during self-appraisal and therefore rate oneself high, it is culturally ingrained in Asians and other Eastern cultures to be modest during self-assessments and therefore rate oneself moderately— likely 5 or 6. Also, the number chosen on the scale is seen by some as an expression of patriotism and therefore tends to be 8, 9, or 10, whereas to others it is an opportunity to make a statement of protest or grievance and therefore tends to be a low number—below 5. In either case, "how satisfied" one is may largely reflect how one feels about his or her country—*not* "how happy." At best, this method measures the respondents' *satisfaction* with their own lives. *Happiness* is *not* what is being measured.

Finland deserves recognition for being crowned the "happiest country" in the world—for the sixth year in a row—although based on an imperfect method of measuring happiness.

Definitely, Finland is one of the wealthiest nations, and perhaps a very citizen-responsive nation—but *not* decidedly or convincingly the *happiest* country in the world. The happiest country could in fact be in Africa, Asia, the Caribbean, North America, South America, or in Europe. The happiest country, wherever it is, should unquestionably have the *highest* percentage of flourishing citizens as well as the *lowest* percentage of languishing citizens. Finland has not met either of these two criteria.

Geographically, the Republic of Finland occupies a total area of 150,928 square miles at the northern edge of Europe with a population of 5.52 million, according to the 2019 census. It is a densely forested cluster of islands (an archipelago) sharing borders with Scandinavian neighbors and Russia. It is the third most sparsely populated country in Europe after Iceland and Norway. It has an average annual income of $49,580. Life expectancy is seventy-eight years for men and eighty-four for women. The country is 90 percent Christians, 56 percent urban dwellers, 44 percent rural dwellers and the literacy rate is 100 percent in every part of the country. Finland is one of the most socially just of all the EU countries and Helsinki, the largest city, is the state capital.

If someday, there is a reason or the need for the UN to find, acknowledge, and crown the happiest living human (HLH) in the world, all eyes will of course turn to the Finns rather than the Afghans or the Lebanese. While on such a mission to find the happiest man or woman, Helsinki (the presumed "happiest city" in the world) will logically be the place to begin the search. One important note of caution is that the happiest living human (or HLH) could very well be in the Bahamas, Barbados, or Antigua—countries with the lowest rate of suicide in the world. Yes, Finland is a lovely country with good governance, decent social services, excellent healthcare, free education, and high average income. Despite these desirable features, Finland also has a high cost of living, long dark cold winters with no sunrise for several weeks in the year, heavy snowfalls, raging snowstorms, high incidence of seasonal affective disorder (SAD), and is number 7 in the use of antidepressants among the thirty-eight member-nations of OECD. The suicide rate in Finland is more than twice the suicide rate in Afghanistan—the declared unhappiest country. It is 6.0 in Afghanistan compared with 13.4 in Finland—according to the WHO 2019 Suicide Report. Consequently, and evidently, every Finn is not automatically a likely candidate for the HLH crown, and every Afghan should not automatically be excluded from consideration.

The smartest human, the fastest runner, the best dressed or best-looking, the wealthiest, the bravest, and the physically strongest among us, can be objectively decided by a panel of neutral judges. *The happiest* among us cannot be similarly selected by a panel because—

A happy man is not what he seems to others but who he seems to himself.
~ Publilius Syrus (85–43 BC)

As a result, we need a valid self-appraising tool for measuring happiness before we can correctly and confidently identify the happiest living human or the happiest country in the world.

Suppose an Afghan citizen trades residence with a Finnish counterpart, neither immigrant could be guaranteed to become the happiest or the unhappiest living human instantly or subsequently. The happiness narrative of both immigrants will certainly be influenced by their newly adopted respective country, but ultimately each individual outcome will depend on *many factors* other than the adopted new country of residence.

Where to Look for the Happiest Living Human

The happiest living human, whether a man or woman, could be somewhere in the Caribbean—where the weather is good all year round, average income is low, but so is the cost of living, social services are not so great, education and healthcare are not free, but the suicide rate is the lowest in the world; or the HLH could be in Northern Europe—where the climate is very severe, average income is high and so is the cost of living, social services are great, healthcare is a right, education is free, and suicide rate is among the highest. According to the WHO Suicide Report of 2018, the top twenty countries with the highest suicide rate in the world are:

1. Lithuania 31.9/100k
2. Russia 31.0
3. Guyana 29.2
4. South Korea 26.9
5. Belarus 26.2
6. Suriname 22.8
7. Kazakhstan 22.5
8. Ukraine 22.4
9. Latvia 21.2
10. Lesotho 21.2

11. Belgium 20.7
12. Hungary 19.1
13. Slovenia 18.6
14. Japan 18.5
15. Uruguay 18.4
16. Estonia 17.8
17. France 17.7
18. Switzerland 17.2
19. Croatia 16.5
20. Equatorial Guinea 16.4

Finland was ranked 23rd with a suicide rate of 15.9 in 2018. The Bahamas was ranked 180th with a suicide rate of 1.7; Grenada was ranked 181st with a suicide rate of 1.7; Barbados was ranked 182nd with a suicide rate of 0.8; and Antigua and Barbuda were ranked 183rd with a suicide rate of 0.5.

The happiest living human may be living his or her happy life anywhere in the world other than Northern Europe. It is absurd to claim that we can rate and rank countries of the world for *Happiness* when there is no validated, universal, and unbiased tool for measuring happiness across nations, cultures, and socioeconomic strata.

What to Look for in the Happiest Living Human

Dylan Graves, science writer and author of *Happier Countries Are More Suicidal: A Look at the World Happiness Report and Suicide* (Medium, 2019), looked at the countries of the world, reviewed the available data from multiple sources about happiness, including the happiness ranking of nations in the World Happiness Report, and insightfully wondered why "happier countries are more suicidal." In the end, he concluded that *Hope* may have a major role to play in *Happiness*. This book, *The Happiness Formula*, shares his opinion. It presents and proposes a new way to measure the happiness of individuals—across cultures and national boundaries—by determining the level of *Hope* and intensity of *Hunger* of respondents, as they actually experience it every day—in *real* life—not in an imaginary or imaginable life.

A life full of *Hope* but with low intensity of *Hunger* is what to look for in the happiest living human. When the level of *Hope* is higher than the intensity of *Hunger*, the ratio of positive emotions to negative emotions is always greater than 1. As will be fully explained in Chapters 11 and 12, this ratio should be highest in the happiest living human.

CHAPTER 2

THE DAWN OF POSITIVE PSYCHOLOGY—BEFORE AND AFTER

T he human pursuit of happiness has been a subject matter of great interest to philosophers for many centuries. Ironically, psychology, the study of human behavior, an academic discipline that grew out of philosophy, showed no interest historically in the subject matter of human happiness. Even as recently as the second half of the twentieth century, improving the lives of untroubled people was of no interest to psychologists. They were exclusively disease focused with all their attention directed at curing mental disorders.

The first significant wave of change in psychology was pioneered by B. F. Skinner and Carl Jung, two *behaviorists* who helped to widen the scope of psychology. Their work shaped the way psychology came to think about human personality, self-development, and habit formation. They promoted the concept of using rewards and punishments to influence, modify, or elicit desired human behavior, but regarded human free will as a delusion with no part to play in shaping human behavior.

Next came Soren Kierkegaard and Jean-Paul Sartre, two *existentialists* who led a movement that popularized the notion of individual responsibility in shaping one's own destiny and finding the meaning of life.

However, it was not until the *humanistic* movement led by Abraham Maslow in the mid-twentieth century that psychology began to entertain a holistic dimension that emphasized that there is an inherent human drive for self-actualization. Maslow was the first to claim that human actions are motivated by certain physiological and psychological needs. In his 1943 article entitled *The Theory of Motivation*, he conceptualized that there is a "hierarchy of needs," and that some needs are very basic and physiological while others are psychological and more complex.

Accordingly, he urged people to first acknowledge their basic needs—such as food, water, warmth, and sleep—before addressing higher needs—such as safety, security, love, esteem and intimacy—and ultimately, seek accomplishments and self-actualization. In other words, first seek the basic needs before progressing to the more complex needs. He helped to advance the concept of promoting psychological health in the absence of psychological disease. In fact, the term "positive psychology" was first coined by Maslow in his 1954 book, entitled *Motivation and Personality*.

When Martin Seligman, in 1996, was elected president of the

American Psychological Association, he adopted the term *positive psychology* as the theme of his tenure and ushered a new era in psychology that shifted away from the traditional focus on human deficiencies, disease, and pain to the proactive promotion of well-being, contentment, and fulfillment of everyday normal people.

Christopher Peterson, a cofounder of the positive psychology movement, defined positive psychology as "the scientific study of what makes life most worth living." As a result, happiness, which Aristotle (2,300 years earlier) had proclaimed "the meaning, purpose, and aim of human existence," became the focus of positive psychologists.

In just twenty years since the movement began, the field of positive psychology grew tremendously. It has inspired research across many academic disciplines with emerging theories, concepts, and conclusions that are finding many applications in the workplace. For example, research shows that when happiness is proactively promoted in the workplace, productivity is increased by 31 percent and innovations go up 300 percent according to the *Harvard Business Review*; turnover is decreased by 51 percent according to Gallup; and absenteeism is reduced by 66 percent according to *Forbes*. Positive psychology research findings are being used in a variety of ways to assess candidates, make hiring decisions, motivate employees, retain, and match individuals to their most effective roles within organizations. With improved understanding of what makes people happy and why, marketing professionals can now tap into the deepest emotions of their consumers to improve sales, CEOs now have better clues on how to improve job satisfaction, and governments are getting better insights on how to plan well-being programs for their citizens. Our overall understanding of human fulfillment, engagement, relationship, gratitude, achievements, and generosity has significantly been improved—thanks to the advent of positive psychology. Despite the considerable enlightenment that positive psychology has brought about in our current understanding of what makes life worth living, there are many questions yet to be answered. Particularly, as one who has been studying human *hope* for decades before and after the dawn of positive psychology, I think that psychologists have too long ignored the role of *hope* in our everyday life. For example:

1. Why do positive psychologists think that happiness (rather than hope) is what makes life most worth living, whereas people without hope are the ones who usually resort to suicide?

2. How is hope related to happiness?

3. Is it possible to have one without the other?

4. Why do humans want to be happy?

5. What exactly does happiness do for *Homo sapiens*?

These are just a few of the many questions answered in the chapters of this book, which introduces a simple equation that makes happiness less elusive, much easier to understand, measure, and monitor.

First, in the following chapter, please allow me to debunk three popular myths about happiness that are untrue.

THREE HAPPINESS MYTHS

I n this chapter, I would like to dispel and debunk three myths about happiness that are seriously misleading and obstructive:

1. Money cannot buy you happiness.

2. Happiness means different things to different people.

3. Happiness is too vague and elusive to measure.

Of these three, debunking the third myth is the principal reason for this chapter and one of the central themes in this book.

Let me point out a personal reflection about the first myth. As far back as I can remember, it always made me happy when my parents, my uncles, or my aunts gave me some money. The same is true for many people that I know. Also, as an uncle to quite a few young men and women—thanks to my siblings—I have found that whenever I give money to any of my nephews and nieces, they seem happy, and it also makes me happy as the giver. Both as a recipient and as a donor, money has indeed bought me some happiness. What money cannot buy me is a happy life.

The second myth is also not true. Happiness does not mean different things to different people. In every culture or language, in Europe, Asia, Africa, Middle East, and Austronesia, there is a word for happiness; although different things may make different people happy, happiness (itself) is an unmistakable feeling of joy, delight, satisfaction, or contentment—to every one of us. We all get happy at various moments and situations in life, irrespective of gender, culture, religion, or geography. Contrary to the rather popular but untrue myth, "happiness does not mean different things to different people." What may mean different things to different people is "a happy life" or that construct that psychologists call *subjective well-being*. Happiness is a fleeting episode of hedonic pleasure whereas a happy life is a sustained and more sustainable overall eudaemonic experience.

I consider it necessary to dispel these two popular myths to help clarify the important difference between *happiness* and *a happy life*. Happiness is a thing whereas a happy life (or subjective well-being) is a construct. The latter has multiple parts or elements that become evident after exhaustive definition or operationalization. One could have some moments of happiness but not an overall happy life; one may have an overall happy life with some occasional moments of unhappiness.

The third myth, which claims that "happiness is too vague and elusive to measure," is, in fact, the acquiescence to intellectual mediocrity and a hasty acceptance of status quo. It is my intent to show beyond any doubt that happiness and/or subjective well-being can indeed be measured. I do not merely disagree that happiness is "too vague and elusive to measure," I am in fact arguing that the reason happiness remains "vague and elusive" is because we have been unable to find a way to measure and quantify it—rather than the other way around. As has historically been true in the history of science, research, and discoveries, when one can measure something, it becomes much easier to show it, feel it, explain it, and demonstrate it. For example, the idea of "normal body temperature" was once a vague and elusive concept; everyday terms like "mild fever" and "high fever" were nonexistent. Until the inventions of Daniel Fahrenheit and Anders Celsius, "fever" as a clinical concept was vague and elusive. The advent of thermometers and the availability of appropriate units of measure (in Fahrenheit and Celsius) made what is now known as the normal body temperatures of 98.6 degrees Fahrenheit or 37 degrees Celsius—possible, less abstract, and real in medical practice. Another example is that historically, no one could tell or affirm who is heavier than whom in a room full of *rikishi* sumo wrestlers until the invention of the weighing scale that made it possible to assign body weights to individuals—by each person simply standing on a device called the *weighing scale*. The concepts of body weight (in pounds (lbs.) and in kilograms (Kg)) and body temperature (in Fahrenheit and Celsius) were in fact *nonexistent* until the appropriate tools and universal units of measure became available. Similarly, we need a valid method and a universal unit of measure to make happiness less vague and elusive.

In conclusion:

1. Happiness is that unmistakable moment of joy, delight, satisfaction, contentment, or peace of mind that any one of us may feel for various reasons in our daily life. The cause or reason for a happy moment may differ but *Happiness* itself is a

universal feeling that is clearly identifiable, and that similarly elicits positive emotions in every *Homo sapiens*.

2. Money can indeed buy you happiness. What money *cannot* buy anyone of us is a *happy life*. The latter may mean different things to different people.

3. Happiness is a real and palpable human feeling—but unfortunately, it is hard to measure and very difficult to quantify. Consequently, it seems vague and elusive.

Next, I have a theory to share with you.

CHAPTER 4

INBORN HUNGER THEORY

A theory is not set in stone. It is an opinion that is offered to explain or make sense out of certain observations and facts that remain baffling.

For example:

- Why is every living human relentlessly in constant pursuit of happiness? In other words, why is happiness a universal obsession of all humans, despite our significant individual differences and unique life circumstances, due to geography, culture, ethnicity, religion, education, gender, income, and lifestyle?

- What does happiness do for *Homo sapiens*? Does happiness have an evolutionary selection advantage?

- When was your very first happy moment in life? How universal is the timing of that experience?

- Where do our human desires come from and what is the first
  desire "expressed" by a newborn infant?

Questions such as these (and more)—that are asking *why, what, when,* and *where* do human desires come from—have been crying out for a coherent theory that could help connect several dots. The existing happiness theories—for example: Hedonism Theory; Desire Theory (Griffin, 1986); Objective List Theory, Authentic Happiness Theory (Seligman, 2003); and the Well-being Theory (Seligman, 2011)—all link personal achievements to happiness.

These theories espouse that happiness is a matter of getting what you want, and they link the fulfillment of one's desire to one's happiness. Every desire theorist agrees that the stronger the desire, the more meaningful the satisfaction received. Also, the stronger an unfulfilled desire is, the worse frustration or sense of deprivation one feels. In common, all these theories have struggled unsuccessfully to explain the origin of human desires. The Inborn Hunger Theory is my attempt to provide answers to the four questions asked above and explain other baffling observations related to happiness and subjective well-being.

Happiness is not a natural human endowment and we as humans are not born naturally happy. In fact, we are all born unhappy: crying, screaming, and kicking as we are forcibly "evicted" from the womb—without prior warning. Happiness must subsequently be earned, triggered, or somehow provoked. Otherwise, our displeasure at birth could conceivably continue without an end.

While we are born unhappy, the Inborn Hunger Theory notes that we are nevertheless pre-wired for happiness by virtue of our five inborn hungers, namely:

- Hunger for inclusion and acknowledgment

- Hunger for intimacy and trusted companionship
- Hunger for food and comfort
- Hunger for information and answers
- Hunger for continuity and certainty

A *hunger,* by definition, is a compelling desire. These five compelling congenital desires with which we are endowed (or saddled as some may say) at birth, push, nudge, and urge us to strive for those things that eventually bring happiness. For example, the hunger for inclusion and acknowledgment urges us to strive for excellence so we can *achieve* or *accomplish* and *become recognized.* The hunger for intimacy and trusted companionship pushes us to associate with others, to love and seek affection, marry, and procreate so we can advance in our *human connections* and *connectedness.* The hunger for food and comfort urges us to plant, sow, hunt, build, or seek employment so we can have *income, food,* and *comfort.* Our hunger for information and answers nudges us to ask questions, seek *knowledge* and *new skills.* Similarly, our hunger for continuity and certainty prods us to seek faith, pray, and pursue salvation—so we can have *continuity, certainty,* and *other reassurances*—in our life.

As the Mega Chart in Chapter 5 and the Big Picture in Chapter 10 will show us, there are five triggers of happiness:

1. Achievements and accomplishments
2. Human connection and connectedness
3. Food and comfort
4. Knowledge and new skills
5. Pleasant spiritual experiences

These five triggers are what make us happy—as consequences of the right response to our inborn hungers.

Precisely, the Inborn Hunger Theory posits that we *all* are born unhappy but pre-wired for a happy life by virtue of our five inborn

hungers that urge, nudge, guide, prod, and prompt us to perform
those acts that ultimately trigger happiness in us.

The Origin of All Human Desires

All our desires in life stem from our five inborn human
hungers—very directly or somewhat indirectly. In other words, all
desires are the modified or unmodified variations of our inborn
human hungers. Due to the influence of culture and the environment,
some of our minute-by-minute desires in life could be wholesome or
immoral, legal or illegal, safe or unsafe, but all of them are variations
of our five inborn hungers. For example, our inborn hunger for food
and comfort urges us *directly* to seek food and shelter; *indirectly* to
seek employment; and occasionally to cheat or steal, embellish and
falsify, but at the end of the day, all human desires (good and bad)
originate from our five inborn human hungers.

The First Episode of Happiness

We all come out of the uterus crying, kicking, and screaming—
unhappy. The very first experience of happiness occurs when we are
wiped dry and clean, wrapped in a warm blanket, cuddled, and fed
milk. With the nipple in the new baby's mouth, the sucking reflex
is automatic. As milk starts to flow, the crying stops and the baby is
"happy" for the *first* time outside the mother's womb. Thus, our first
experience of happiness, as humans, occurs soon after birth—when
food and comfort are given.

In the nursery, the new baby is usually asleep and comfortable
with a full stomach. Time passes and the baby wets itself and is
hungry once again ("unhappy"), triggering it to cry. When the caregiver changes the diaper and/or feeds the baby, the baby becomes
"happy" once again and stays quiet, sleeping, or awake.

Apparently, the *first* primal demand (or desire) of any newborn human infant is for *food and comfort*, which also can be regarded as the trigger of the very first episode of "happiness" in any human life.

Inside the Womb vs. Outside the Womb

During the first ten months of life while inside the womb, all that babies know and become accustomed to is *comfort and good well-being*. Objectively, this fetal well-being is routinely and frequently confirmed by the obstetrician during bio-physical profile (BPP) evaluation using ultrasonography (Williams, Obstetrics, 2014). The common finding in most pregnancies is a BPP score of 10/10 that (to

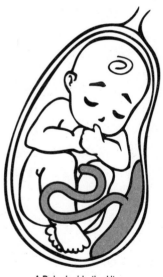

the obstetrician) indicates a perfect *fetal well-being score*. Naturally, the sudden or abrupt expulsion from the womb (or uterus) is unwelcome by a baby who has been experiencing a desirable well-being inside the uterus prior to delivery.

Who wouldn't want to live in a place where food flowed freely, the atmosphere was warm, serene, and comfortable, and stress was nonexistent? No wonder that during moments of severe deprivation or in times of extreme physical and emo-

A Baby Inside the Uterus

tional distress, humans at any age tend to assume the so-called "fetal position," suggesting an intuitive or subconscious desire to return to that most protective posture once assumed in the uterus.

According to the World Health Organization report, globally more than 800,000 people take their own lives by suicide every year.

Interestingly, the highest rate of suicide in every region of the world occurs among fifteen to twenty-five-year-olds—the exact age range when demand for individual responsibility is usually on the rise whereas extrauterine adaptive skills remain still relatively immature. If going back to the uterus were a practical option, there are many who would choose to do that rather than take their own lives.

In general, it could even be speculated that the instinctive or subconscious desire to return to the uterus or stay close to it could be one of the reasons why all children (young or old, male or female) tend to hang around their mothers, rather than their fathers.

Why Is Every Human in Pursuit of Happiness?

As we discussed, every newborn baby (upon evacuation from the uterus at birth) is immediately encumbered with five inborn hungers. These hungers prompt infants to cry—either because they are hungry, uncomfortable, or lonely. Young children do the same and then ask questions and seek inclusion—all of which are necessary for survival. All human efforts after birth are entirely in response to the five inborn human hungers; all our pursuits (including the pursuit of happiness) are intuitive, primal, and obligatory because of the existential value of *happiness.*

Our five inborn hungers, serving as prompts, urge us to do the appropriate things required for survival and to flourish. During infancy and early childhood, mitigation of these five inborn hungers is all that is necessary or required for a feeling of satisfaction and subjective well-being—because children are "nowians" whose concerns are only about *now.* In adulthood, by contrast, we become "futurians" and, as Daniel Gilbert (2005) puts it, "At some point between our high-chairs and our rocking-chairs, we learn about later" (and therefore are always thinking of tomorrow). Consequently, as adults, our preoccupation and obsession about the future renders the mere mitigation of our inborn hungers insufficient to earn us contentment. *Hope*, being the only effective antidote for uncertainty, remains an absolute requirement for our happiness as we become adults.

Research findings by Chida and Steptoe (2008), Boehm, et al. (2015), and the Harvard Human Flourishing Program (2019) show that happy people have better than average blood pressure readings, a stronger immune response, fewer cardiovascular complaints, a higher level of satisfaction with life, and a longer life expectancy—confirming the *existential value of happiness*. Happiness is a primal desire and a congenital obsession of all humans because we need it to survive, to succeed, and to flourish. Through natural selection, as *Homo sapiens* we have become consciously, unconsciously, intuitively, obligatorily, and genetically pre-wired for happiness for reasons of survival and self-preservation.

Without our five inborn hungers as prompts, our survival outside the uterus would be impossible.

CHAPTER 5

THE TRIPLE-H EQUATION

Historically, I became interested in the study of *human hope* because I was under the assumption that this is what made life worth living—since people without *hope* often took their own lives. This was prior to the advent of positive psychology and *happiness* was not a popular subject as it is today.

Among the major findings that I had made during the three decades of studying human hope were the following.

Finding Number 1

There are five (real or potential) human assets available to each of us.

These assets are:

1. Intrinsic assets

2. Human family assets

3. Educational assets

4. Economic assets

5. Spiritual assets

We derive that thing we call hope from these five assets. Those who are the richest in these five essential human assets (as they are also called) are the people fullest of hope.

Finding Number 2

There are five inborn human hungers with which we are all saddled from the moment of birth and throughout the whole of our life.

These hungers are:

1. Hunger for inclusion and acknowledgment

2. Hunger for intimacy and trusted companionship

3. Hunger for food and comfort

4. Hunger for information and answers

5. Hunger for continuity and certainty

And our response to these five inborn hungers largely determines how we feel, what we do, or how we react.

In the year 2000, after "happiness" had become the focus (and mantra) of the positive psychology movement, I became interested in the scientific study of human happiness—wondering how hope and happiness are possibly related.

I then conducted extensive international surveys, during which participants were asked to list three occasions, events, or situations in their personal lives that made them very happy. From these surveys, it became clear that there are in fact only five principal triggers of happiness:

1. Achievements and accomplishments

2. Advancements in human connection and connectedness

3. Increase in income and personal comfort

4. New knowledge or newly acquired skills

5. Pleasant spiritual experiences

As I was reviewing and comparing the five sources of human hope, the five inborn human hungers, and the five triggers of happiness juxtaposed on a large chart as shown below, I made a discovery.

THE MEGA CHART

I	II	III
THE FIVE SOURCES OF HUMAN HOPE	**THE FIVE INBORN HUMAN HUNGERS**	**THE FIVE TRIGGERS OF HAPPINESS**
Intrinsic Assets [your ego strength, and natural attributes]	Hunger for inclusion and acknowledgment	Achievements, victories, triumphs, and accomplishments
Human Family Assets [help, support, and assistance from others]	Hunger for intimacy and trusted companionship	Advancement in human connections and connectedness
Economic Assets [your sense of material adequacy and sufficiency]	Hunger for food and comfort	An increase in income, material possessions, and personal comfort
Educational Assets [what you know and how much you know]	Hunger for answers and information	New knowledge and new skills or capabilities
Spiritual Assets [your faith, religious beliefs, sense of right and wrong, and notion of life after death]	Hunger for continuity and certainty	Pleasant spiritual events or experiences

Three surprising relationships became instantly apparent to me:

1. The five triggers of happiness and the five sources of human hope are contextually related and highly suggestive of correlation.

2. The five triggers of happiness are, in essence, the desired solutions (or answers) to the five inborn human hungers.

3. The five sources of human hope (or assets) and the five inborn human hungers are basically the opposite sides of the same coin.

It was a eureka moment and the most accurate phrase or language that I could find to precisely express these fascinating relationships was a mathematical one—in the form of a very simple equation that says, $\frac{HOPE}{HUNGER} = HAPPINESS$.

This equation, which I later dubbed the Triple-H Equation, was essentially implying that:

1. *Happiness* is best assured when *Hope* is high and *Hunger* is low.

2. When *Hope* is high, it lessens the pain of *Hunger*, and when *Hunger* is overwhelming, it dampens the feeling of Hope.

3. *Happiness* is not possible in the absence of *Hope*.

4. No one can possibly have a happy life when *Hunger* is overwhelming.

5. A happy life is essentially a life that is full of *Hope*.

6. True contentment is only possible when *Hunger* becomes negligible and insignificant.

If we think of happiness as a feeling of joy or satisfaction, the face validity of this equation is apparently very strong since hunger should unquestionably decrease happiness while hope is naturally expected to increase happiness. Humans as "futurians" are heavily obsessed about the future and there is no better antidote for the uncertainties of tomorrow than *hope*—the feeling and the belief that all will be well.

Beyond this face validity, literature overview and empirical analysis of Pleeging, Burger, and J. van Exel (2019) show a strong positive relationship between *Hope* and *Happiness*; Everett Worthington Jr. (2020) has demonstrated that more hopeful people are indeed happier and healthier than unhappy people. Also, the Triple-H Equation is well corroborated by the Desire-Fulfillment Theory of Chris Heathwood (2014), which holds that the fulfillment of a desire (or hunger) results in happiness. The Human Flourishing Program findings of Harvard University, Ruut Veenhoven's Opentia Newsletter 3(2015), and T. C. Bailey, et al. (2007) all corroborate the Triple-H Equation. Martin Seligman's PERMA model and Tal Ben Shahar's SPIRE theory both cite relationship, spirituality, and knowledge, three well-known sources of human hope, as determinants of happiness.

Experientially, we all know that a hopeful disposition usually makes one feel happier, and a happy feeling strengthens our hope for the future, whereas unfulfilled desires make us unhappy. How we perceive the future greatly affects how we feel in the present and in fact, during a very successful and flourishing life, one's subjective feeling of well-being can drop precipitously the moment we receive news that the future will be grim and bleak—for example, at the news of a fatal medical diagnosis.

If we deconstruct the Triple-H Equation with *Hope* and *Hunger* exhaustively defined, broken down, and rigorously analyzed, *Happiness* becomes much easier to comprehend, explain, and even measure. As such, without further delay, let us now begin the process of deconstructing the Triple-H Equation by defining and breaking down each of its three variables—starting with *Hope*.

LET'S TALK ABOUT HOPE

What is hope?

Where does hope come from?

Why do you need hope?

How can you boost your hope?

How hopeful are you today?

According to evolutionary biologists, Ryan Gregory (2009), Oliver Riepell (2010), and others, *Homo erectus* was the first human ancestor to acquire the ability to stand and walk upright on two legs. This evolutionary advancement granted him the use of two hands for making tools, hunting, and manipulating his environment more effectively. Much later, when *Homo sapiens* (the successor of *Homo erectus*) acquired the frontal lobe (of the current human brain), this significant advantage over *Homo erectus* granted him and his descendants (i.e., us) the ability to mentally peek into the future, dream, imagine, and visualize things that are not yet a part of reality—and thus, *the capacity to hope was born.*

Hope is a belief and the feeling that one's aspirations are achievable or that what one desires is also possible based on one's own appraisal of all personal *assets* that are perceived as available. Hope is more than a mere desire, imagination, or a daydream. It informs us, it assures us, and it motivates, strengthens, and energizes us to perform. When hope is high, your fears, your worries, and your doubts significantly diminish—resulting in a state of informed courage. From this informed courage emanates the energy for action. Hope has a cognitive, an affective, and a motor component that combine to make hope a practical tool for everyday human survival. In other words, hope takes knowledge and understanding, it involves feelings and emotions, and it requires actions and execution (or actual doing).

According to my research findings, there are five sources from which we derive hope:

1. The number one source of hope is your own self, your ego strength, virtuous attributes, signature strengths, self-discipline, and self-esteem—collectively called your *intrinsic assets.*

2. The second source of hope is your family, friends, colleagues, and others around you from whom you expect and get support, love, empathy, and understanding—collectively called your *human family assets.*

3. The third source of hope is your own sense of material sufficiency, perceived resource adequacy, and available (real or potential) buying power—collectively called your *economic assets.*

4. The fourth source of hope is your personal intellect, experience, skills, level of curiosity, knowledge, and awareness—collectively called your *educational assets.*

5. The fifth source of hope is your own core beliefs and personal ethos, prayerfulness, moral tenets, ethical convictions, spirituality, and religious faith—collectively called your *spiritual assets.*

These five categories of (real or potential) assets constitute the five sources of your hope, and they are also known as the five *essential human assets.* When these assets are boosted or high, your hope is enhanced. Simply put, high hope results when your intrinsic assets, human family assets, economic assets, educational assets, and spiritual assets are high.

Here is a true story—of an unintended human experiment—that illustrates what hope is, why we need it, and where it comes from:

On August 5, 2010, thirty-three miners became trapped in a gold mine in the country of Chile following an accidental explosion and consequent collapse of the walls of the mine. Immediately, these miners became completely cut off from contact with the outside world and the rest of humanity. They became helplessly confined about half a mile deep underground without any means of communication with family and friends. It was sweltering hot—92°F—and they were not prepared for an extended stay in the mine, with only two days' worth of emergency food and water. They had no idea how long their ordeal would last at two thousand feet below the surface of the Earth and, along with the heat and hunger, they were mostly in the dark. The miners needed to preserve their helmet lamps and the heavy equipment they could alternatively use would contaminate their air supply.

Under such grave uncertainty and harsh conditions, the miners began to wonder if the Chileans had given up on them by assuming that they had all been killed. Even if they tried to hold on to the positive notion that they could and would be rescued, the thought of not knowing how long and when or how they could be ultimately rescued must have been so tormenting after twenty-four hours, forty-eight hours, or seventy-two hours of absolute uncertainty. A whole week went by followed by a second week without any communication with the outside world. By this time, the plight of the men had captivated people around the globe, but no one had any idea whether all—or any—of the thirty-three miners were even still alive.

With my deep interest in the subject of human hope, I personally began to wonder how these miners could be coping if, in fact, they were still alive. Were they hopeful or in despair? If in despair, what were they doing to themselves or to one another; and if not in despair, what were they possibly doing to cope and keep hope alive while in such absolute state of uncertainty—and possibly impending death?

Luckily, after seventeen days, the first contact with the outside world became possible—and more importantly all the thirty-three miners were reported to be alive. It was a real tale of human survival and a rare opportunity for the ultimate validation of my published findings about human hope—made thirty years earlier. The Chilean rescue site headquarters itself, appropriately enough, was nicknamed Camp Hope by the Chilean people.

"We knew if we broke down, we would all be doomed. Any time a different person took a bad turn, everyone rallied around to try and keep up the morale," later recalled Mario Sepulveda, one of the rescued miners.

From the accounts of the miners themselves, the hope they needed came from:

1. Individual courage and willpower
2. Togetherness and assistance from one another
3. Good stewardship of the very limited resources
4. The harnessing of available knowledge, skills, and expertise
5. Spiritual faith and prayer

All of which affirmed that intrinsic assets, human family assets, economic assets, educational assets, and spiritual assets are indeed the five sources of human hope.

According to all accounts, the miners chose hope over despair and did the following:

- Right from the beginning, they realized the need to work together as a family of thirty-three with emphasis on common good, personal responsibility, and individual relevancy. As a result, there emerged a collective attitude of excellent cooperation with strong solidarity among the men aged nineteen to sixty-two. In accordance with the spirit of equality, they took a vote to decide everything they did; interestingly, the tally of almost every vote they took (as the miners later recounted) was unanimous. As a result of their singularity of purpose, there was collective strength, courage, and willpower to work together and stay alive.

- They emphasized a collective approach for solving every problem and organized a system of support for individual emotional needs. Mario Gomez, the oldest of all the miners, set up a buddy system to constantly look out for one another regardless of age. They held daily group meetings to support

one another, undeniably a good show of human family
support.

- Recognizing the important issue of sustenance and the need
  for continued food availability, foreman Luis Urzua took
  personal responsibility for food rationing. Extreme rationing
  became imperative because the total food supply was low and,
  more importantly, some food needed to always be available
  in order to preserve a continuing sense of food availability
  despite actual insufficiency and shortage. Starting from day
  one, each miner received two small spoonfuls of tuna, a bis-
  cuit, and a sip of milk every two days from Luis. This prudent
  stewardship was a noteworthy display of skillful management
  of resources to extend the duration of food availability despite
  severe insufficiency.

- Individual expertise and special personal skills (available
  within the group) were harnessed and put to use for the
  common good of everybody. For example, nineteen-year-old
  Jimmy Sanchez (the youngest of them all) was designated the
  environmental engineer for the group because of his personal
  disposition. Jose Henriquez, a very religious individual, was
  placed in charge of giving the daily sermons, and he also led
  prayers. Edison Pena, the "electrician," wired up a series of
  lamps that provided eight to twelve hours of light every
  twenty-four hours to simulate night and day. These examples of shared wisdom and exchange of expertise among the
  miners constituted a boost of the overall educational assets.

- All thirty-three miners had regular group prayer sessions as
  well as frequent sermons. Specifically, Jose Henriquez, serving
  as the spiritual leader, gave daily sermons to address issues of
  faith in the face of uncertainty. Individual contemplations as

well as private thoughts of spiritual reconciliation also went on, such as forty-four-year-old Esteban Rojas's vow during the ordeal to formally wed his live-in girlfriend in the proper manner of the church if he ever got out alive. What a show of individual faith and a boost to the collective spiritual assets of the thirty-three miners during the ordeal.

These activities went on for seventeen days in the face of absolute uncertainty—without the knowledge of an impending rescue. On October 13, 2010, the whole world watched in real time on television and cheered as all thirty-three miners were pulled out one by one from the belly of the Earth, after a total of sixty-nine days—with every one of them looking healthy. Indisputably, these men survived because they had *hope* and were therefore able to cope.

In every respect, the Chilean miners' saga was an incidental double blind human study (or an unplanned experiment) it confirmed beyond any doubt the five sources of human hope. Individually or collectively, we all need hope to cope with the stress of life and high hope can be accrued and/or maintained by boosting your five essential human assets—intrinsic assets, human family assets, economic assets, educational assets, and spiritual assets.

The capacity to hope is the most significant fact of life.
It provides human beings with a sense of destination
and the energy to get started.
~Norman Cousins

EXERCISE 1
How Hopeful Are You?

Your hope score is a measure of how hopeful you are. To determine your hope score, the PISA Hope Scale is provided below with instructions.

PISA Hope Scale

Instructions

To determine your hope score, please read each of the six statements below. On a scale of 1 to 8 (with 1 indicating not true at all and 8 indicating very true), circle the number that best represents your response to each statement. In other words, after reading each statement, circle 1 or 2 if the statement is not true at all, circle 3 or 4 if it is somewhat true, circle 5 or 6 if it is true, and circle 7 or 8 if it is very true.

Statement 1
Generally speaking, I am an optimist.

1   2   3   4   5   6   7   8

Statement 2
I do believe I have something to offer to others in this life.

1   2   3   4   5   6   7   8

Statement 3
In case of an emergency, I have someone I can count on.

1   2   3   4   5   6   7   8

Statement 4
When I need answers, I am usually successful finding them.

1   2   3   4   5   6   7   8

Statement 5
Considering the resources available to me, I am more fortunate than many.

1   2   3   4   5   6   7   8

Statement 6
When I think about my relationship with God, I feel reassured and less afraid.

1   2   3   4   5   6   7   8

Interpretation

The arithmetic sum of all the circled numbers is your PISA hope score. Hope scores range from 6 to 48. A score of 48 represents the highest score possible. A hope score of 36 to 48 is the desirable range, and it represents a healthy optimistic outlook. A hope score of 35 and below needs improvement. Hope scores below 25 indicate a pessimistic tendency that needs to be addressed. Hope scores of 6 to 12 require immediate intervention.

Please, save your hope score for use in a later exercise contained in this book.

CHAPTER 7

THE FIFTEEN TENETS OF HUMAN HOPE

The fifteen tenets of human hope are a body of facts, inferences, impressions, and conclusions that I have arrived at after thirty years of research, surveys, studying, interviewing others, and thinking about human hope. Each of the tenets articulates and addresses one important aspect of the very complex issue of life, hope, and optimism.

In the preamble and tenets 1 through 6, you are asked to pause and reflect on the aspect of hope just addressed. The questions posed are to provoke your reflections.

The Preamble

The universe is as baffling as human life is mysterious, and no one knows with absolute certainty the origin and purpose of life or of the awesome universe where humans live and try to thrive. Because of all the unanswered questions, humans, human life, and the universe remain enduring mysteries despite science and religion.

Pause and reflect: Do you really know with absolute certainty how, why, and from whence you came or where exactly you shall return after death?

The First Tenet: Hope Is What Gives Meaning to Life

For all of us, life remains a poorly understood human journey. Its exact beginning is unknown, the duration is left to speculation, and there is neither an apparent mission nor a destination. Fundamentally, were it not for the ability to hope, human life would have no meaning at all.

Pause and reflect: How meaningful would your own life be if you had no hope or the belief that your desires, goals, expectations, and aspirations will someday be realized?

The Second Tenet: Hope Is the Courage to Live

The mysteries of life are the root causes of human restlessness. Every individual human is under the yoke of daily stress that stems from the consequent uncertainties of a poorly understood life and purpose of life. From these uncertainties emanate all our fears and insecurities that require that personal courage called hope.

Pause and reflect: Why do we need courage if fear is not an issue in our life? Why do we need self-esteem if self-doubt is not a problem? Why do we desire to know if ignorance is good? Why do we have the need to love and be loved if others do not matter? Why do we save and hoard if our future is so certain? Why do we pray if we have all the answers?

The Third Tenet: Humans Are Resilient Because We Can Hope

The love of self has no limit, and each of us is first and foremost a self-advocate. Intuitively, we therefore want to thrive and survive. We yearn, compete, and struggle best when we have hope. When we try and don't succeed, we try and try again—but only if there is hope.

Pause and reflect: Who is number one in your life? What wouldn't you do for yourself? What keeps you going? Why do you try again and again until you succeed?

The Fourth Tenet: Peace of Mind Comes from Hope

Peace of mind is a priority of every human, and it is hope that gives rise to peace of mind. Without the former, the latter is impossible. Humans therefore cling to hope because of its promise of personal peace. When we have hope, we are less afraid of the future, and the inner peace of mind that ensues (which some call happiness) is the foundation of human contentment.

Pause and reflect: Is a happy life possible without peace of mind? Can one have peace of mind when the future is full of doubts and uncertainties? Why do we find immediate relief at the sight of the proverbial light at end of the tunnel? Why does a pay raise make one happy even before receipt of the larger paycheck?

The Fifth Tenet: Hope Is Both a Feeling and a Belief

Hope is the feeling that what is desired is possible. It is also the belief that a given goal is indeed achievable. In other words, hope has cognitive and affective components. All thoughts, beliefs, and feelings that help to reduce the stress of life ultimately contribute to hope. We have hope when we believe and feel that all will be well. When you strongly believe and feel passionately enough, action is bound to follow.

Pause and reflect: What are your feelings about tomorrow? What are your beliefs about next year? What one thing are you planning to do today? Do you believe and feel it is achievable?

The Sixth Tenet: There Are Five Sources of Human Hope

There are five essential human assets without which life becomes meaningless, unbearable, and eventually unsustainable. These five *essential* human assets are *the five sources of human hope*. They are as follows:

1. **Intrinsic assets (or ego strengths):** These are the signature strengths and virtuous attributes of an individual that constitute the core of his or her personality, make all adaptations possible, and serve the primary functions of ensuring self-gratification as well as personal survival. When a person is rich in intrinsic assets (or high in ego strength), he or she has a feeling of reasonable wellness—both inward and outward—with a sense of personal fitness, a high degree of self-esteem, willpower, and a profound degree of personal courage. When there is poverty in intrinsic assets, it often appears as a general sense of worthlessness, a feeling of incapability, or a lack of personal relevancy.

   - **The best-known single method (BKSM) for boosting one's own intrinsic assets is to seek and find a life purpose, a**

meaningful goal, or one's true calling. When you find your true calling, your signature strengths ensue and the best in you comes out.

Pause and reflect: Think of a time when you were full of inner strength and personal courage and your self-esteem was very high. What factors contributed to that experience or feeling?

2. **Family assets:** These are your perceived availability of moral support, empathy, love, inspiration, and other signs of recognition or help, which we sense in the process of interactions with the immediate family, relatives, friends, colleagues, neighbors, and significant others. When a person is rich in human family assets, he or she has evidence of empathic understanding, love, respect, and the reassuring approval of family, friends, colleagues, and significant others. When we are poor in human family assets, there is a feeling of personal isolation and loneliness as well as a sense of being of no consequence in the community to which one belongs.

   - **The BKSM for boosting one's own human family assets is to recognize the needs of others and remain considerate of those around you.**

Pause and reflect: If you were to suddenly become unavailable and instantaneously unreachable by anyone and everyone, who (and how many people) will sincerely miss you and why? How would it make you feel not to be missed when you are away, and not to be wanted when you are around?

3. **Educational assets:** These are all the forms of awareness and knowledge we have acquired through formal and informal learning (or by experience), which provide a better

understanding of the environment, our immediate plight, and the laws of nature or society. When someone is rich in educational assets, he or she is confident about the adequacy of personal knowledge or expertise and remains reasonably assured that relevant answers are within reach. When someone is poor in educational assets, there is a feeling of information deficit, a perceived lack of answers to important questions, and/or the absence of relevant knowledge sufficient to allay our prevailing fears and anxieties.

- **The BKSM for boosting one's own educational assets is to increase your curiosity and learn something new every day.**

Pause and reflect: Have you ever had an "aha!" moment upon finding an answer to a disquieting question? What exactly was that feeling about? And what about the confidence and the sense of empowerment that you feel when debating a subject matter that you have read about and have thoroughly researched? Doesn't knowledge make you feel powerful?

4. **Economic assets:** This includes money and property, real or anticipated, including all items, arrangements, or situations that contribute to your personal wealth and sense of material sufficiency either because these things actually enhance your potential buying power or merely confer a perceived relative degree of financial/material comfort. When a person is rich in economic assets, he or she has a reassuring sense of material sufficiency and financial contentment based on the perceived adequacy of money, food, and shelter or other material resources. When someone is poor in economic assets, there is an increased degree of anxiety over money as well as

a heightened sense of *perceived* material insufficiency, regardless of the real personal financial net worth in dollars.

- **The BKSM for boosting one's economic assets is to first and foremost appreciate and value what you already have, therefore count your blessings and market your skills.**

Pause and reflect: If you could have all the money you want, how much would you ask for? One thousand dollars, one hundred thousand, one million, or a billion? What would you do with such an amount? How much money do you think is just enough to give you inner peace and satisfaction? Are you sure of your answer?

5. **Spiritual assets:** These consist of the benefits, advantages, and peace of mind that you enjoy because of your religious faith, beliefs, and practices. These are the dividends of your spirituality that come from your personal notion of God and man; life and death; good and evil; right and wrong; souls and spirits. When a person is rich in spiritual assets, he or she has a strong sense of being blessed, favored, and protected by something cosmic and omnipotent. The opposite is true of someone that is poor in spiritual assets and who therefore bears the heavy burden of life's uncertainties alone—without expectations for divine assistance.

- **The BKSM for boosting one's spiritual assets is to be mindful of death and frequently ask yourself these questions, "Why am I here?" and "How do I want to be remembered?"**

Put together, *hope* is personal courage, affirmed and strengthened by knowledge, supported and nourished by the family, reinforced by a sense of material sufficiency, and accompanied by spiritual faith.

Pause and reflect: What would you do if you were diagnosed with a disease that would bring profound uncertainty into your life? Would you go into denial, ignore, and repress the information, or summon up courage to deal with the situation? Would you ask, wish, or expect others to help and support you? Would your available resources, such as personal financial status or medical insurance, become relevant as you try to plan and cope? Would you derive comfort from the fact that you have the means to pay your medical bills? Would you pray for your plight, seek spiritual strength, and possibly ask for divine assistance? Would you ask questions, seek advice from experts, and look for information wherever? In other words, would you reach for hope? How and why?

The Seventh Tenet: Hope Has Four Characteristics

Human hope is *dual* in nature, *neutral* in character, *constant* in its presence, and *transmissible* from person to person. Hope is dual because it has two sides or faces. It is neutral because anyone (both the good and the bad) can have it. It is constant because everyone always has some. It is transmissible because it can be shared and passed on.

The Eighth Tenet: Hope Is Dual in Nature

There is always more than one side to hope. It is both a universal human attribute and yet very personal. Hope is often the reason for consensus and unity—among people, communities, or nations—but is also frequently the cause of dissension and discord when there is a clash of hopes. Consequently, *divergent hopes* are the cause of every interpersonal dispute, sibling rivalry, interethnic quarrel, and

international war, while *convergent hopes* are the bases of mutual
goal commitment, international peace, and sustained coexistence.
Hope can make you smile and also make you cry—as we all often
shed tears of joy.

The Ninth Tenet: Hope Is Neutral in Character

Human hope is morally *neutral* in character, meaning that hope
is neither right nor wrong. Regardless of personal character or moral
standing of the individual, anyone can have hope. Hope is not exclusively reserved for the righteous, the strong, the weak, or the wealthy.
It is a common human attribute that intrinsically does no harm. It
motivates everyone and helps everyone in their individual pursuits,
regardless of the righteousness of the intended goal and the legality
or illegality of the endeavor being hopefully pursued. Hope is always
neutral, and anyone can have it.

The Tenth Tenet: No One Has Zero Hope

Some amount of hope is *constantly* present in each of us although
the quality and amount may vary from person to person. No human
can be totally hopeless since every deliberate human action or activity requires some amount of hope for execution. No functioning
living human can have zero hope. As the saying goes, "If there is life,
there is hope."

The Eleventh Tenet: Hope Is Transmissible

Human hope is *transmissible*, meaning hope can be shared or
passed from one person to another—vertically (as from parents
to children, mentor to mentees, or speaker to members of an audience) and horizontally (as colleagues to colleagues, friends to
friends, or one member to another in a support group). Hope is most

successfully transmissible when there are unifying issues, common concerns, or similar beliefs between the giver and the recipient of hope. Thus, the transmission of hope is faster and easier between like-minded people or in a community of people with convergent desires and aspirations.

The Twelfth Tenet: Hope Begets Hope

Every previous achievement informs and suggests more possibilities to us. More possibilities expand our dreams. As our dreams grow and widen, we become even more hopeful—because hope begets hope.

The Thirteenth Tenet: Humans Always Reach for Hope

In response to stress, especially when severe, all humans reach for hope by various means available, according to personal characteristics and individual styles. The urge to reach for hope may come intuitively or deliberately. It may be spontaneous or may evolve gradually. Some of us reach for hope calmly, gracefully, diplomatically and with civility. Others, through hostility, violence, or confrontation. How each of us sees the world, reacts to stress, or cries out for help, is ultimately determined by our own unique individual nature and nurture. Reaching for hope is what we all do—because we must, and we love to.

The Fourteenth Tenet: There Are Optimists and There Are Pessimists

Depending on our own unique individual nature and the type of nurturance we have received from parents and mentors, each of us becomes either mostly an optimist or largely a pessimist in the way we see the world and live our lives. Optimists see and emphasize the brighter sides of things, while pessimists have the tendency to emphasize or give the least favorable interpretation to events and outcomes of the past, the present, or the future. To the optimist, the future is therefore full of hope, whereas to the pessimist, it is full of hunger. These are two views of the same world interpreted according to our nature and upbringing.

The predisposition for optimism is largely an acquired characteristic, a perception of a future that registers at the high-hope end of the hope–despair continuum. The tendency for pessimism (also a learned behavior) is rooted in a belief that the future, even at its best, will always fall short of expectations. If a particular goal remains unachieved after only a few attempts, an optimist is most likely to make further attempts, while the pessimist is more likely to give up the pursuit more quickly and entirely. Additionally, when a goal is ultimately determined to be truly impossible to achieve, the optimist is likely to modify the goal and keep hope alive rather than give up on hope. Despite the differences between an optimist and a pessimist, neither is without some hope—and some doubts.

The Fifteenth Tenet: Boosting Human Hope Requires SORKS

In other words, it takes Self-efforts, Others, Resources, Knowledge, and Soul to accrue and boost human hope. As the SORKS-phenomenon shows, this is the priority of every living human. (See the box that follows).

The **SORKS** Phenomenon

As part of the initial research investigation about human hope, my collaborators and I did two telephone surveys in 1979, asking people to tell us what the word *hope* meant to them personally—in one word or two words. At the time there were no cell phones, and our telephone callers—using the old voluminous telephone directories of the time—simply dialed hundreds of home phone lines by random selection. The age and gender of the respondents who answered the phone did not matter and were never asked. When children answered, they were asked to call an adult to the phone. To our great delight, we had enough respondents who answered our survey positively. Most were in fact very gracious, and they gave their answers to our question—in one word or two—as was requested. There were of course some declinations but very few. Subsequently, we wanted more information and so we did a second survey, but this time using an open question. We asked—"Please, what can you tell us about human hope?" To our great disappointment a high percentage of the people we randomly contacted this time—unlike before—declined to participate for various reasons. Interestingly, however, from the reasons they gave for having no time to participate in our survey, we fortunately gained a wealth of unsolicited information about the most common priorities and preoccupations of people—as indicated by our survey decliners. In our follow-up investigations on our initial finding, we were able to confirm that peoples' concerns,

preoccupations, priorities, obsessions, and aspirations re-
volve around five issues and five issues only:

1. Issues of Self
2. Issues of Others
3. Issues of Resources
4. Issues of Knowledge
5. Issues of the Soul

In other words, the daily worries, aspirations, motives,
hungers, and concerns of all of us, though quite diverse and
seemingly countless, ultimately pertain to these five recurring
issues or subject matters:

- Matters of *self* or self-interests—such as personal
  health, safety, survival, longevity, and well-being
- Matters involving *others*—such as relationships, al-
  truism, cooperation, empathy, competition, or rivalry
  within the family, the workplace, and the community in
  which we live
- Issues of *resources*—such as money matters, adequate
  housing, food, transportation, and material possessions
- Issues of *knowledge*—such as personal intellect, education, awareness, and the quest for information and
  answers
- Matters of the *soul*—such as faith in God, personal
  salvation, life after death, religious beliefs, and spiritual
  ethos

Though these findings first emerged purely by accident,
we realized that our endeavors had indeed led to something

profound, and hence I named this very fascinating revelation—the "SORKS Phenomenon."

As noted above, the acronym S-O-R-K-S stands for self, others, resources, knowledge, and soul to highlight the five categories of issues that predominantly preoccupy all humans in our everyday life. For example, every day, you wake up, make your bed, brush your teeth, do your physical exercise, take a shower, get dressed, eat breakfast, and take your medicine—all matters of *self* and *self*-interest.

You exchange ideas with your colleagues, give and receive feedback, write a memo, reply to e-mails, make phone calls, send text messages, cooperate with your spouse, compete with your rivals, attend funerals, keep your doctor's appointments, visit a sick friend, and attend your cousin's wedding—matters involving *others*.

You commute to work, negotiate with your boss for a pay raise, cash your checks at the bank, shop for a new car, buy groceries, pay your bills, close business deals, invest in stocks, and rent or buy from vendors—all issues of *money* and *resources*.

You seek answers, listen to news, ask questions, review documents, read a book, look for information, attend classes, go to meetings, or attend conferences—all issues of *knowledge*.

To maintain a good relationship with God or Allah, or Yahweh, you may go to church on Sundays, mosque on Fridays, or temple on Saturdays, attend Bible study every Wednesday, give thanks, count your blessings, pay your tithes, say your prayers, and contribute to charity—all matters of the *soul*.

There are, of course, some daily activities that straddle more than one category of issues but invariably, any log, diary, or chronicle of human daily activities, when carefully analyzed, will confirm that the SORKS phenomenon is indeed real. Living a life of hope is about living a well-balanced life, in which one can appropriately be self-centered and yet quite altruistic, adequately resourceful and highly knowledgeable as well as sufficiently spiritual. Such a homogenous blend of SORKS activities is what paves the way for success and fulfillment in life. Your hopes, your hungers, and your happiness are all consequences of SORKS. And hence, it requires SORKS to boost human hope.

The Last Word

Universally, life is unpredictable, and every person is burdened by the yoke of uncertainties, insecurities, and hungers (whether inborn, acquired, acute, chronic, minor, or major). Unless there is enough of that human attribute we call hope, many of us soon succumb to the stress of daily life, becoming depressed and even distressed. Hope is the reason we humans have been able to tolerate a life imposed on us, for an indefinite duration, without our consent, a clear purpose, or a known mission.

Due to our capacity to hope, we humans have successfully dared and are thriving in an awesome universe that is as baffling as life is mysterious. Hope is the essence of human life and without it, life is meaningless and unbearable—in fact, inconceivable.

WHAT ABOUT HUNGER?

- What is hunger?
- Where does hunger come from?
- What does hunger do to you and for you?
- How hungry are you?

As humans, we have many desires and aspirations, and the term *hunger* is reserved for a compelling desire or a burning aspiration. Some desires are inborn whereas others are acquired or learned. The most consequential of all desires are the five inborn human hungers, as already discussed in Chapter 4. They are:

1. Hunger for inclusion and acknowledgment
2. Hunger for intimacy and trusted companionship
3. Hunger for food and comfort
4. Hunger for information and answers
5. Hunger for continuity and certainty

These hungers are regarded as inborn because infants and very young children spontaneously express them without being taught or prompted by adults. These facts came to light when my students and I decided to chronicle what primal demands infants and toddlers universally make. The objective of the study was to observe and document what spontaneous actions and primal behaviors infants and very young children demonstrate—without any prompting by adults—starting from the moment of birth. The aim was to find out—based solely on observed behavior—what human infants and very young children truly seem to intuitively want, pursue, demand, and desire insistently. To achieve this goal, we chronicled the primal demands of newborn infants and the spontaneous desires of toddlers including the behaviors of three- and four-year-olds. In so doing we found, documented, confirmed, and concluded the following:

1. During delivery (or parturition), almost every baby comes out of the womb apparently in discomfort and usually crying, kicking, and screaming. It was also remarked that the crying and kicking (both of which are truly primal and spontaneous) promptly stopped once the babies were wiped dry, kept warm, cuddled, and fed—a plausible suggestion that infants do desire or demand *food* and *comfort*. While in the newborn nursery and for several months after discharge from the hospital, infants were noted to cry mostly when they were wet or *hungry*, confirming an inborn desire for *food* and *comfort*. Crying usually stops once infants are fed and/or their diapers are changed.

2. Starting from about six to eight months of age, as documented by multiple observers, including pediatricians, parents, and nannies, babies show a preference for one

particularly "trusted person" (often the mother or a nanny) in whose arms they prefer to remain and cuddle. It was remarked that infants would often cry endlessly in protest until handed over into the arms of their own preferred caregiver— suggesting a desire or a demand, on the part of each infant, for a *trusted* and a particularly preferred *companion*.

3. As confirmed by multiple observers—including parents, grandparents, and older siblings—once they can talk, children generally ask a lot of questions. Apparently, there is so much for them to learn and understand. "What is that, Grandma?" is often followed by a "Why," then another "Why?" or "How?" or "When?" Even before they can speak and ask questions, babies and infants reveal their curiosity by looking around, pointing to things, or reaching for a rattle or other object that is placed in front of them. Verbalized and nonverbalized queries of children demonstrate beyond any doubt their strong "desire to know"—suggesting an inborn hunger for *information* and *answers*.

4. Whether it's time to play or to do chores, observers reported countless anecdotes attesting to the fact that children (unless autistic or not feeling well) love to be included. At school they hate "time-outs" and bitterly protest any forms of involuntary exclusion, as often expressed in common complaints such as "Mom, they won't play with me" or "they won't let me help." Also well documented by multiple observers is that children commonly crave recognition—as in "Daddy, Daddy, see how strong I am" or "look, Grandpa, I did it all by myself!"— because of their strong desire and hunger for *inclusion and acknowledgment*.

5. Also evident from multiple documentation by observers, is
   that children seem to love repetition and would frequently request encores, as in "Daddy, let's do that again, please"—right
   after the second or even the third ride on a merry-go-round
   at the park. There is often "Grandma, tell me another story"
   at the conclusion of one, two, or three previous bedtime
   stories—on the same night. It was also remarked by several
   observers that a game of "peek-a-boo" with a child could go
   on forever if the adult participant would only fully cooperate,
   because children love *continuity*. Equally as much, they also
   like the feeling of *certainty* and can be very "unforgiving"
   when promises are broken—"Grandpa . . . but you promised,"
   they would protest in distress. In what amounts to open so-
   licitations, children (according to parents) often ask, "Am I a
   good boy, Daddy?" "Am I a smart girl, Mommy? or "Will I be
   strong like you when I grow up?"—all of which suggest children's strong desire for *reassurance*, their love for *continuity*,
   and a hunger for *certainty*.

6. Interestingly, there was just one isolated report by a daycare
   employee who observed a three-and-a-half-year-old child
   making the "sign of the cross" before eating her lunch. This
   observation turned out to be an outlier finding, with no cor-
   roboration from other observers. The little girl's parents were
   Catholics who always prayed before meals as a family. Our
   conclusion was that it was a learned or taught behavior rather
   than a primal act or evidence of a "spiritual instinct."

Beyond childhood, as we grow from infancy through puberty
into adolescence, early adulthood, middle age, and finally old age,

our inborn hungers persist and continue to have a major influence on what we do and how we feel. Our five inborn hungers contribute largely to the stress in our lives, but they also serve as useful reminders or prompts that urge us to take appropriate actions for our own survival and well-being—as already theorized in Chapter 4.

We do what we must do as well as what we love to do because of our inborn hungers.

For example, we strive for achievements, personal excellence, and distinction at the urge of our hunger for recognition; we engage in collaboration, friendship, love, and marriage in response to our hunger for intimacy and trusted companionship; we work hard to get money so we can attend to our hunger for food and comfort; we seek knowledge and education because of our hunger for answers and information; we pray for long life, and even life after death, perform physical exercise, buy health insurance, and seek warranties— all at the urge of our hunger for continuity and certainty. Every action that we take as humans (individually or collectively) is provoked by our inborn hungers.

What Our Hungers Do to Us and for Us

From the moment of our birth, through infancy, early childhood, adolescence, adulthood, old age, and until death—regardless of culture, language, gender, or geography—our five inborn hungers serve as natural prompts, nudging and urging us to take those actions that make survival, well-being, and contentment possible. Accordingly, these five inborn hungers persist throughout our life span, though they may vary in intensity during different phases of the human life cycle. These hungers are therefore not optional aspirations but universally endowed, necessary, compulsory, and permanent. Our

inborn hungers have existential value but when they become too severe and/or overwhelming, happiness (or a happy life) is impossible.

Everything that we do (individually or collectively) is provoked
or inspired by our five inborn hungers. We compete, seek excellence,
or distinction; we collaborate, make friends, seek love and affection,
or companionship; we work, plant and sow, slog, and toil; we read,
learn, investigate, and explore; we are prayerful and religious, eat
well, and stay physically fit—all in response to the urges and nudges
of our five inborn hungers.

As a matter of fact, the origin, purpose, and evolution of human
cultures, institutions, and inventions—such as the internet, radio,
television, cell phones, schools, universities, medicine, hospitals, law,
religion, parliament, law, space exploration, marriage, sports, education, journalism, farming, agriculture, information technology, ar-
chitecture, home construction, city planning, commerce, home, car,
life, and health insurance, industrial revolution, inventions such as
airplanes, trains, and automobiles, the printing press, conflict resolutions, binding arbitration, gender equality, civil rights, and other
human advancements in scientific research, space exploration, ar-
chitecture, engineering, and religion—were all inspired and insti-
tuted in response to our five inborn human hungers. In fact, human
civilization itself is a consequence of our collective response to our
inborn human hungers.

The Airport Experiment

In 1980, I coached five adorable-looking and hard-to-resist
young Boy Scouts to help me carry out a survey at the old National
Airport located in the suburbs of Washington, DC—now known as
Ronald Reagan International Airport.

In that survey, which was conducted many years before 9/11 and the subsequent strict airport security rules, travelers waiting for their flights were individually approached at random by uniformed Scouts, with paper and pencil in hand, who had been coached to politely ask: "Sir (or Madam), may you please tell us for what reason you are traveling today?"

Upon review and careful analysis of the responses gathered, every reason the travelers gave had something to do with either responding or reacting to one or more of the five inborn human hungers. For example, some travelers were "going on vacation," others "going to visit" someone relevant in their life, "for business," "family reunion," "going back to school," "job interview," "travelling with a church group," "to receive an award," "to attend a wedding," or "going to a seminar."

The result from this experiment confirmed the fact that every traveler interviewed at the airport on that day was doing something directly or indirectly related to one or more of his or her five inborn hungers. The same will be true if you stand at a busy intersection and ask everyone passing by where they are going and why.

*Our desires define us more than
any other aspect of our lives.*
~Harrison Barnes

EXERCISE 2:
How Hungry Are You?

Your hunger score is a measure of how hungry you are. To determine your hunger score, the Hunger Scale is provided below with instructions.

PISA Hunger Scale

Instructions

To determine your hunger score, please read each of the six statements made below. On a scale of 1 to 8 (with 1 indicating not true at all and 8 indicating very true), circle the number that best represents your response to each statement. In other words, after reading each statement, circle 1 or 2 if the statement is not true at all, circle 3 or 4 if it is somewhat true, circle 5 or 6 if it is true, and circle 7 or 8 if it is very true.

Statement 1
I am currently under a lot of stress.

1   2   3   4   5   6   7   8

Statement 2
I do not get the respect that I deserve.

1   2   3   4   5   6   7   8

Statement 3
I have no trusted or intimate companion.

1   2   3   4   5   6   7   8

Statement 4
Lack of enough money is a constant worry of mine.

1   2   3   4   5   6   7   8

Statement 5
I have so many unanswered questions.

1   2   3   4   5   6   7   8

Statement 6
I am worried about my future.

1   2   3   4   5   6   7   8

Interpretation

The arithmetic sum of all the circled numbers is your PISA hunger score. Hunger scores range from 6 to 48. A hunger score of 36 to 48 represents severe hunger. A hunger score of 18 to 36 represents moderate hunger and a hunger score of 6 to 18 represents low hunger. A hunger score of 6 is the least hunger score possible, and the most desirable.

Please, save your hunger score for use in a later exercise.

CHAPTER 9

THAT THING WE CALL *HAPPINESS*

What Is Happiness?

Happiness is the feeling of joy, delight, satisfaction, well-being, fulfillment, or contentment. It is a state of emotional well-being that a person experiences momentarily because of a specific event, or more broadly as a result of positive self-appraisal. Overall, happiness is a consequence of our own thoughts, actions, reactions, perception, judgment, and conclusions—all in the context of the prevailing internal and external factors of everyday life.

Accordingly, there are myriad factors that determine your happiness, such as genetics, emotions, engagement, relationship, achievements, income, spirituality, knowledge, memories, current experience, desires, and aspirations.

The Triggers of Happiness

Over the years, I have given lectures and speeches to several professional organizations and multiethnic civic groups in North America and in West Africa. I often gave out blank sheets of paper to all the attendants or participants and asked them to write down for me three things, occasions, or events that have happened to them in their lives that made them very happy. Upon reviewing and analyzing thousands of these responses from men and women in various walks of life, the following became evident:

Although there are innumerable determinants of happiness, there are five principal triggers of happiness:

1. Personal achievement, a victory, or an accomplishment
2. Advancement in personal relationship, human family connections, or connectedness
3. Increase in income, material possessions, and personal comfort
4. Acquired new knowledge or new skill, expertise, or capability
5. A pleasant spiritual experience, event, or occurrence

In other words, there are only five categories of situations in life that routinely trigger happy feelings in us—although each category may have multiple contributory factors.

These triggers work by boosting our essential human assets and by lessening the intensity of our inborn hungers. In other words, they work by increasing *hope* or by decreasing *hunger*—since $\frac{HOPE}{HUNGER} = HAPPINESS$.

A happiness *trigger* is only effective in provoking the feeling of happiness by resolving a problem, answering a desire, or mitigating a hunger. However, the form, the type, the duration, and the depth of the resulting happiness depends on the import, significance, and relevance of the problem solved, the hunger fulfilled, or the desire realized.

For example—a thirty-five-year-old female attorney, who finds a good and free parking spot (just in time) on a very busy downtown street, is *happy* for not being late to an appointment with the city administrator. The same woman successfully gives birth to a set of twins (one boy and one girl) after three years of struggling with infertility. She is once again *happy* but much *happier* than finding a good parking spot downtown. These two instances of emotional pleasure, while similarly positive for this attorney, are *not* qualitatively equivalent in significance, depth, or gravity. In each instance, happiness was triggered because a problem was solved, a desire was realized, or a hunger was mitigated. However, the duration, intensity, type, and form of the ensuing happiness depends on the significance and the intensity of the problem solved, the desire realized, or the hunger answered.

There are two major types of happiness:

1. When the joy being felt is purely a momentary feeling of raw pleasure, enjoyment, or comfort, this type of happiness is called *hedonia*. A good example of hedonic happiness is what you feel as you drink a glass of your favorite wine, or when you reach a sexual climax (or have an orgasm).

2. On the other hand, if the joy being felt is a feeling of overall well-being, life satisfaction, or contentment, that kind of happiness is called *eudaemonia*. Eudaemonic happiness is what you feel when you get married, get a pay raise, buy a new car, or move into your dream house.

Hedonic happiness is fleeting, transitory, short-lived, temporary, and of little consequence, whereas eudaemonic happiness is longer-lasting, more enduring, and far more consequential. The former is about *here* and *now*. It is about pure enjoyment, and raw pleasure, whereas the latter is about purpose, growth, and the future. "Happiness" as used in the *Triple-H Equation* and throughout this book connotes overall happiness—a combination of hedonia and eudaemonia.

How Can We Measure Happiness?

How to measure happiness has been a problem for research scientists, clinical psychologists, economists, and more recently, policy makers—all of whom are interested in quantifying happiness for different reasons. Primarily, they want to be able to measure it, detect changes, and make comparison possible. Happiness, being a subjective emotional feeling, currently lacks a universal tool for objective and valid quantification. The only person who knows how happy you are is you—and only you. Consequently, only you can accurately describe how happy you feel—but only qualitatively since happiness has no standard unit of measure. Any interviewer who wants to know how happy you are must ask you the open-ended question, "How happy are you feeling?" Alternatively, the interviewer may ask you specific questions using survey tools such as the 1 to 10 Happiness Scale, Subjective Happiness Scale, Oxford Happiness Questionnaire, the Yale Happiness Test, or the Penn Authentic Happiness Survey and Test. All these tools ask specific questions that require yes or no answers and sometimes require indications of your degree of agreement or disagreement with specific statements in the questionnaire. Currently, there is no universally acceptable unit of measure for happiness that allows direct comparison among individuals across cultures and socioeconomic strata.

Measuring happiness has been very challenging but not impossible—especially if you choose to use the Triple-H Equation. For example, in my professional practice as a family physician and as a professional coach, I routinely calculate what I call the Personal Happiness Index (PHI) of every patient or client that I see. I do this by simply dividing the client's hope score by his or her hunger score. In my clinical practice, the determination of the patient's PHI is just as important and routinely determined as the blood pressure, body temperature, pulse, and body mass index (BMI).

PHI is the mathematical ratio of *hope* to *hunger*. The former generates positive emotions whereas the latter generates negative emotions. Consequently, PHI reflects the ratio of your positive emotions to your negative emotions. In Exercises 1 and 2 respectively in Chapter 6 and Chapter 8, if you calculated your Hope Score and Hunger Score, you can now determine your PHI.

Let us now look at the big picture and connect all the dots.

THE BIG PICTURE

As you may remember, in Chapter 2, after reviewing the history of positive psychology, I raised the issue of why positive psychologists have given very little attention to the subject of human hope despite the strong relationship between hope and the "will to live." In Chapter 5, the Triple-H Equation asserted that, and in the subsequent chapters, we deeply examined the three variables in this equation. Specifically, in Chapters 6 and 7, we talked about hope, its five sources, its fifteen tenets, and its role in human daily life. In Chapter 8, we discussed the five inborn human hungers including what they do to us and do for us. Finally, in Chapter 9, we learned about the five triggers of happiness.

In this chapter, we'll put together all the different pieces of information we've covered to give the "big picture." As you can see in Figure A, the Triple-H Equation is deconstructed with its three variables precisely defined and broken down into their elements. In Figures B and C, the sources of human positive emotions and negative emotions are illustratively delineated. Figure D illustrates the common pathway or "the why and how" the triggers of happiness work—to ultimately result in the generation of positive emotions (or happiness). Combined, Figures A, B, C, and D give the big picture, a comprehensive summary of the human happiness narrative.

Box 1   **Figure A - Triple H Equation [deconstructed]**

HOPE is a belief and a feeling that one's own desires and aspirations are indeed achievable. Your hope comes from you and your five essential human assets. These five assets are:

1. **Intrinsic Assets** [i.e., your ego strength, self-esteem, and other virtuous attributes or characteristics]
2. **Human Family Assets** [i.e., the love, help, support, and assistance from others]
3. **Economic Assets** [i.e., your income, savings, material possessions and overall sense of material sufficiency or resource adequacy]
4. **Educational Assets** [i.e., your intellect, awareness, skills, knowledge, and curiosity]
5. **Spiritual Assets** [i.e., the benefits and dividends of your faith, spirituality, and religious beliefs]

These assets (which may be real or potential) are the **FIVE SOURCES OF HUMAN HOPE.**

$$\frac{HOPE}{HUNGER} = HAPPINESS$$

Box 2

HUNGER is a compelling desire or a burning aspiration. The most compelling of all hungers are the **FIVE INBORN HUMAN HUNGERS.** These inborn hungers are:

1. Hunger for inclusion and acknowledgment
2. Hunger for intimacy and trusted companionship
3. Hunger for food and comfort
4. Hunger for information and answers
5. Hunger for continuity and certainty
These five hungers are the primary drives and motives behind every action we take in life.

Box 3

HAPPINESS is that unmistakable feeling of joy, delight, satisfaction, fulfillment, or contentment that one gets at various points or moments in life. There are five life situations that are known to trigger the feeling of happiness in us. These five *triggers* of **HAPPINESS** are:

1. Personal achievements, victories, and accomplishments
2. Advancement or enhancement in personal relationships, human family connection, or connectedness
3. Increase in income, material possessions, and personal comfort
4. Acquired new knowledge, new skill, expertise, or capability
5. Pleasant spiritual experiences, events, or occurrences (e.g., Baptism, first communion, pilgrimages, religious revivals, initiation, or induction)

TRIPLE H PROJECT LLC

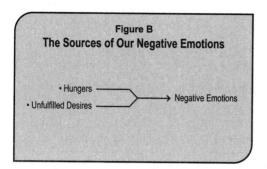

Figure B
The Sources of Our Negative Emotions

• Hungers
• Unfulfilled Desires ——→ Negative Emotions

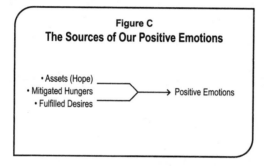

Figure C
The Sources of Our Positive Emotions

• Assets (Hope)
• Mitigated Hungers ——→ Positive Emotions
• Fulfilled Desires

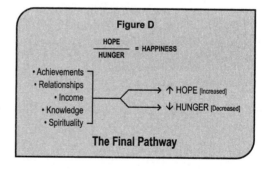

Figure D

$$\frac{HOPE}{HUNGER} = HAPPINESS$$

• Achievements
• Relationships
• Income
• Knowledge
• Spirituality

↑ HOPE [Increased]
↓ HUNGER [Decreased]

The Final Pathway

Figure A basically shows a deconstructed Triple-H Equation. It asserts and reiterates that happiness ensues when there is a rise in HOPE and a decrease in HUNGER. Figures B and C respectively identify the sources of our negative emotions and positive emotions. And figure D explains that a rise in assets (HOPE) and/or a reduction in HUNGER is what ultimately triggers happy feelings in us.

Figures A–D combined, the big picture, gives a precise summary of the relationship among HOPE, HUNGER, and HAPPINESS. It shows us how this relationship works, and why it works. For example, it provides us the answers to several fundamental questions—such as:

- What is it that makes people happy, and *why*?
- What is it that makes people sad, and *why*?
- What is a happy life?
- How can happiness be best measured?

Let us start with the first question:

What Is It That Makes People Happy, and Why?

According to the big picture (see Box 3)—there are five major situations in life that make people happy:

1. When people achieve, win, or accomplish something;
2. When people make advancements in personal relationships in any way;
3. When there is a rise in income, material possessions, and personal comfort;
4. When new knowledge or a new skill is acquired; and
5. When a pleasant spiritual event or religious experience occurs.

For the purpose of clarity, let us consider each of these five situations separately—one by one.

Achievements

In positive psychology, achievement is well recognized as a determinant of happiness. It is the "A" in Martin Seligman's PERMA model of happiness. What is largely absent in the literature is the plausible explanation for why (or how) achievements trigger happiness in people. *Why* is the student who made the soccer team happy? *Why* is the athlete who wins a gold medal at the Olympic Games happy? And *why* is the journalist who is awarded a Pulitzer Prize happy? Yes, achievements trigger happiness in all of us, but the unanswered question is how and why exactly does an achievement make you a happier person?

ANSWER:

The link between achievement and happiness has to do with hope and hunger. When you achieve, win, or accomplish a goal, you are proud of yourself, and your self-esteem rises. *Self-esteem* (as defined in Box 1) is an intrinsic asset and when intrinsic assets rise, hope rises. Additionally, when your self-esteem rises, your craving for acknowledgment is correspondingly lessened—which means a decrease in your inborn hunger for inclusion and acknowledgment (see Box 2). With a boost in hope, and a decrease in hunger, happiness is triggered because positive emotions are generated as shown in figures C and D. For example, Allen, a seventeen-year-old high school student, got a perfect score on the SAT. This *achievement* gave a big boost to Allen's self-esteem—and therefore an increase in his intrinsic assets. The boost in intrinsic assets raised his level of hope. The intensity of his inborn hunger for inclusion and acknowledgment became lessened by virtue of having been confirmed, acknowledged, and included among the best by the SAT report. With an increase in HOPE and a decrease in HUNGER, HAPPINESS was triggered because: $\frac{\text{HOPE}}{\text{HUNGER}} = \text{HAPPINESS}$.

Relationships

Positive psychologists regard the relationships one has with others as the most important determinant of happiness. *Relationship* is the R in Martin Seligman's PERMA. What is yet to be explained is why and how positive relationships trigger happiness. A brother who finally reconciles with his estranged sister is happy; two old friends who reunite after a long period of separation are happy; and a young lady who gets engaged is happy. Yes, positive relationships make people happy but *how* and *why*?

ANSWER:

The link between positive relationships and happiness has to do with increased HOPE and decreased HUNGER. Positive relationships boost your human family assets and consequently your hope increases (see Box 1). Also, when your human family assets are boosted, your inborn hunger for intimacy and trusted companionship is proportionately mitigated (see Box 2). With a rise in HOPE and a fall in HUNGER, HAPPINESS is triggered. Very illustrative is the case of Zelda, a young lady who received a marriage proposal from her boyfriend. It was a boost to Zelda's human family assets and therefore a rise in hope. It also answered her inborn hunger for intimacy and trusted companionship. With a rise in HOPE and mitigation of her HUNGER, HAPPINESS is triggered because $\frac{\text{HOPE}}{\text{HUNGER}} = \text{HAPPINESS}$.

Increased Income

An increase in income makes people happy or happier but how and why?

The answer to this question is provided in the story of Marcus, an assistant manager in a production factory who got a substantial raise in salary. The *increase in income* gave a boost to his economic assets and therefore a rise in hope. The increase in income made food and comfort more affordable for Marcus and therefore his financial insecurities and food anxieties decreased. With a rise in HOPE and a decrease in HUNGER, HAPPINESS was consequently triggered. This was how and why Marcus became happier, since $\frac{HOPE}{HUNGER} = HAPPINESS$.

New Knowledge and Skills

The acquisition of new knowledge and new skills makes people happy. For example, take Helen, who just got licensed as a pilot and can now fly an airplane on her own, without supervision. Like the four-year-old who finally learns to ride a bicycle without the training wheels; the teenager who gets an official driving license; or the nursing student who becomes certified as a registered nurse (RN), Helen was happy to become a certified pilot. The acquired new knowledge, new capability, and skill gave a boost to her *intrinsic assets* and her *educational assets* and therefore a rise in her hope. Additionally, her hunger for recognition and acknowledgment lessened due to higher self-esteem. With a rise in HOPE and a decrease in HUNGER, HAPPINESS was triggered.

Pleasant Spiritual Experience

Pleasant spiritual experiences, for example, baptism, first communion, pilgrimage, religious induction, initiation, or revival, make people happy because these experiences boost spiritual assets and consequently, HOPE. With increased assurance of salvation (or life after death), one's inborn HUNGER for certainty and continuity become lessened in intensity.

Virginia, a nurse with whom I worked many years ago, was a self-proclaimed "born again Christian." One summer, she and twenty-five other friends traveled to the state of Israel with a pastor who baptized them in the river Jordan. Upon her return to work,

Virginia expressed how much happier she was due to her baptism in the biblical river. She apparently became more assured of her salvation and life after death. The boost to her spiritual assets led to a rise in hope. Also, her inborn hunger for continuity and certainty became less intense. With a boost in HOPE and mitigation of HUNGER, she became much happier following her pleasant spiritual experience in Israel.

In summary—as the cases of Allen, Zelda, Helen, Marcus, and Virginia illustrate and confirm—what makes people happy are personal achievements; positive human relationships; an increase in income or material possessions; knowledge or new skills; and pleasant spiritual experiences. Fundamentally, however, it is the rise in HOPE and a decrease in HUNGER that ultimately triggers HAPPINESS.

Importantly, the form, the type, the duration, and the depth of the happiness felt depends on the significance or relevance of the assets boosted and the intensity of the hunger mitigated. When you find the lost key to your car, you are happy but much happier when you finally get that dream promotion you have been wishing for at your workplace. These two instances of emotional pleasure, while similarly positive, are *not* qualitatively equivalent in significance, depth, or gravity. In each instance, happiness was triggered, because a *problem* was solved, a *desire* was realized, or a *hunger* was mitigated. However, the duration, intensity, type, and form of the ensuing happiness depends on the significance and the intensity of the problem solved, the desire realized, or the hunger answered.

What Is It That Makes People Sad and *Why*?

Inarguably, unhappiness (or sadness) is brought about when there is a loss or deprivation. Two very good examples are the *loss* of a loved one due to death and the *deprivation* of income due to unemployment. The harder questions to answer are *how* and *why*? In other words, what is the exact mechanism by which the loss of a loved one or the deprivation of employment brings on unhappiness?

ANSWER:

The loss of a loved one decreases your human family assets and consequently results in a decrease of HOPE. Additionally, such a loss intensifies your hunger for intimacy and trusted companionship. With a decrease in HOPE and a rise in the intensity of your HUNGER, unhappiness (or sadness) ensues. Similarly, the loss of employment decreases your economic assets, which means a decrease in HOPE, and additionally, your inborn hunger for food and comfort intensifies proportionately. With a decrease in HOPE and a rise in HUNGER, HAPPINESS decreases because $\frac{HOPE}{HUNGER} = HAPPINESS$.

As the "Big Picture" illustrates, there are five inborn human hungers and five essential human assets. When our assets are increased and/or our hungers are decreased, positive emotions ensue; whereas when our assets are decreased and our hungers are intensified, negative emotions result.

Unhappiness (or sadness) ensues when there is a decrease in assets and a rise in hunger as often happens due to any tragedy such as a tornado, hurricane, earthquake, fire, accident, flood, diagnosis of cancer, and other adversities. A perfect example is the COVID-19 pandemic that disrupted life and caused human unhappiness all over the world—individually and collectively.

Using the COVID-19 pandemic as a case study of human unhappiness, let us briefly explore *why, how,* and *what* brings unhappiness into our lives:

On January 1, 2020, nothing seemed unusual as the clock struck midnight. People in Times Square reveled, danced, and toasted to new beginnings as they made resolutions for the year—an expression of *hope* and *happiness* about the future. Before long, the COVID-19 infection that began in China started to spread very quickly to other countries—resulting in a worldwide pandemic. In order to slow down the spread of this highly infectious and fatal viral infection, *social distancing* became the singular recommendation by the infectious disease world experts. For social distancing to be truly effective, human gatherings were initially discouraged and subsequently prohibited. As a result, every workplace—except hospitals, pharmacies, grocery stores, and the post office—had to be shut down in the United States. I personally was self-quarantined at home, and all the daycare centers, barber shops, schools and colleges, restaurants, churches, temples, and mosques were closed. As a result of all these shutdowns, most people were literally out of work. The general advice was to keep at least six feet away from one another whenever possible. Due to the suspected pattern of spread and the higher fatality in senior citizens, visits to grandparents by their grandchildren were specifically discouraged. The all-day news on TV was full of reports of rising death rates, inadequate hospital beds for the sick, and the scarcity of protective equipment for the doctors and nurses. Because of panic buying and hoarding, many shelves in the stores became empty. Items such as sanitizers, gloves, masks, toilet paper, canned food, and bottled water were rationed or unavailable for purchase. There was no effective cure for the COVID-19 infection, and the possibility of vaccines was said to be at least eighteen months away. Everyone was instructed to remain indoors and not to leave the house except when it was absolutely necessary. As a result of these disruptions caused by the COVID-19 pandemic, there was a prevailing feeling of unhappiness—worldwide.

The Genesis of COVID-19-Related Unhappiness

If one looks through the prism of the Triple-H Equation, the COVID-19 epidemic has basically done two things to bring about worldwide unhappiness: 1—It has intensified our inborn human HUNGERS; and 2—It has diminished our essential human assets (or sources of HOPE).

For instance:

- *Social distancing* discouraged human gatherings for entertainments, marriage ceremonies, funerals, and religious worships—intensifying our inborn human hunger for inclusion as well as diminishing our human family assets.

- The shutdown of workplaces and the consequent unemployment diminished our economic assets, raised our financial anxieties, and intensified our inborn human hunger for food and comfort.

- Because very little is known about the origin of COVID-19, its routes of transmission, exact incubation period, possible cure, and effective prevention, there are many questions and our inborn human hunger for answers and information intensified. Also, because all the schools closed for a year or more, formal education via face-to-face classroom instructions diminished the continuous accrual of educational assets for many.

- The indefinite duration of the pandemic (not knowing how long it was going to last) intensified our inborn human hunger for certainty. Also intensified was our fear of death, our desire for long life, and therefore the intensification of our inborn hunger for continuity and longevity.

- Overall, our five sources of HOPE (intrinsic assets, human family assets, economic assets, educational assets, and spiritual assets) were all under assault during this pandemic. Likewise, our inborn HUNGERS (for inclusion, intimacy, companionship, information, answers, food, and certainty) intensified during this pandemic.

Thus, the unhappiness associated with the COVID-19 pandemic was due to a decrease in hope and a rise in hunger. Yes, the virus COVID-19 caused the pandemic disease, but the associated global unhappiness is a "hope and hunger" issue. There was unhappiness because HOPE decreased and HUNGER intensified.

What Is a Happy Life?

As the big picture indicates, each one of us has five (real or potential) assets and five inborn hungers. When our assets are flourishing and we are therefore full of Hope, a happy life is what results, but if our hungers are overwhelming, life can become very miserable. No life is exclusively full of hope and completely devoid of hunger. Every individual life is a mixture of both hopes and hungers, positive emotions and negative emotions, some good times and some bad times. In other words, no life is exclusively full of intrinsic assets, human family assets, economic assets, educational assets, and spiritual assets without some number of hungers, some unfulfilled desires, unanswered questions, and some unrealized goals.

Since no life is perfect, a happy life is not supposed to be perfect. A happy life is a life where there is something to love, something to do, and something to look forward to. It is a life with more hope than hunger, more positive emotions than negative emotions, more good days than bad days. A happy life is a life that is full of hope, despite the disappointments of yesterdays, the imperfect circumstances of today, and the uncertainties of tomorrow.

How Can Happiness Be Best Measured?

The best and easiest way to measure happiness (knowing what we know now) is to simply determine the ratio of hope to hunger—as the Triple-H Equation instructs. In other words, divide your HOPE score by your HUNGER score. The two macro-determinants of our HAPPINESS are our HOPE (or assets) and our HUNGER (or compelling desires). Each of us has a highly individualized set of life circumstances that ultimately determine our own characteristic assets/hungers ratio called Personal Happiness Index (PHI). Your PHI is the mathematical ratio of your HOPE score to your HUNGER score and it constitutes a true measure of your HAPPINESS—since $\frac{HOPE}{HUNGER} = HAPPINESS$. If your HOPE score is 32 and your HUNGER score is 26, your PHI is 32/26 (1.230). Your hope and hunger scores come from your own self-assessment on the Hope Scale and Hunger Scale, respectively. When your PHI is greater than 1.0 (e.g., 1.230), it means that your hopes outweigh your hungers. This classifies you as a happy person but not as happy as the person with a PHI of 3.166. It is uncommon for two people to have an identical PHI.

The information needed to determine the PHI of an individual is obtained through self-reporting and self-appraisal. The respondent simply answers twelve questions—six items about Hope (or assets) and six items about Hunger. The questions require answers with room to indicate the degree of agreement or disagreement on a Likert scale of 1 to 8. There are no questions about income, level of education, marital status, age, gender, race, national GDP, or system of government in the country of residence. PHI is truly a *personal* happiness index of the individual. It is ideal for monitoring individual improvements after clinical interventions, and it makes it possible (for the very first time ever) to compare and rank individuals across cultures and national boundaries—regardless of socioeconomic differences. This new way of measuring happiness will be discussed in the next chapter in more detail.

CHAPTER 11

A NEW WAY TO MEASURE AND QUANTIFY HAPPINESS

s I write, there are no known hormones or neurotransmitters found in human blood, urine, or saliva that can be measured as biological markers of happiness. Using the frequency of smiling or laughing and other behavior, as correlates of happiness, are also unreliable methods of measuring happiness. One reason is that using the frequency of smiles and laughter as a measure of happiness is culturally biased against people of Eastern upbringing who are generally taught or raised to show little or no overt emotions in public. Consequently, any true measurement of happiness requires self-appraisal rather than behavioral markers.

Self-appraisals, however, are not entirely problem free. Particularly flawed are those self-appraisal questionnaires and surveying tools that are used for tracking global happiness trends—where the respondents are asked about things such as their annual income, level of education, marital status, national GDP, system of governance, and other unproven determinants or correlates of happiness.

Current Tools for Measuring Happiness

Most of the different tools that are currently in use for measuring happiness are at best only helpful in differentiating "very happy" individuals from "very unhappy" individuals. They are of little benefit when trying to characterize those respondents who are in between these two extremes. Consequently, these tools are not good for monitoring progress and measuring the outcomes of interventions—such as coaching and counseling. Some of these questionnaires contain culturally biased items and therefore are inappropriate as tools for global surveys across continental boundaries. Other questionnaires are difficult to administer, score, and interpret because of the length, style, and content of the questionnaires. Some, like the Cantril Scale (aka Cantril Ladder) used by Gallup in its global surveys and by a wide variety of researchers as their tool for well-being assessments, instruct respondents to rate themselves on a Likert scale of 0 to 10. Generally, tools such as this are good for identifying the very happy (scores of 9 and 10) and the very unhappy (scores of 0 and 1). The question is—what does a score of zero mean? Does it mean complete absence of all positive emotions? Does a score of ten mean absolute contentment with no room or need for further improvement? Are all the people who rate themselves as five on the ladder exactly happy to the same degree in reality?

Although all these flaws and limitations are not applicable to every tool in use today, all the tools in use today are less than ideal for monitoring individual progress clinically, or for comparing and ranking individuals—across cohorts, cultures, and national boundaries.

Fortunately, things may be about to change because by virtue of the Triple-H Equation, it has become possible to routinely measure and quantify happiness by simply dividing the hope score of any individual by his/her hunger score as the equation instructs. The resulting answer is called Personal Happiness Index (PHI). Hope score and hunger score come from one's own self-assessment on the PISA Scale (aka the Edo Questionnaire).

About the PISA Scale and PHI

The PISA Scale is a twelve-item questionnaire. Six of the twelve items are about hope and the other six are about hunger. The scale can be self-administered or dispensed by an interviewer (with the help of an interpreter if necessary). The PISA Scale is free of cultural biases, and it focuses on universally applicable human issues of hope and hunger. It therefore is an ideal tool for global surveys. There are no questions asked about annual income, marital status, level of education, national GDP, or system of governance. The PISA Scale measures each respondent's level of hope and intensity of hunger. Since hope generates positive emotions and hunger generates negative emotions, PHI is, in essence, the ratio of positive emotions to negative emotions. The PISA Scale has been heavily tested and clinically used in the United States, Canada, Ghana, Nigeria, and Jamaica. It has good internal consistency with an alpha value of 0.88; content validity ratio is 0.85—with five SME used in calculating the CVR; and test-retest reliability is 0.95. In other words, statistical studies show that the PISA Scale is a valid and reliable scale for measuring happiness.

PHI, which is easy to determine after the twelve items on the PISA Scale have been answered by the respondent during self-appraisal, can identify who is happy, very happy, unhappy, very unhappy, flourishing, or languishing. As shown in the interpretation guide below, when PHI is greater than 1.0, the respondent is considered a "happy person" and a PHI of less than 1.0 defines "unhappiness." PHI of 4.0 or greater defines a "flourishing individual" and PHI of 0.250 or less defines a "languishing individual." PHI is never zero and it can be as high as 8.0. However, there is no specific score that is the highest possible flourishing score. PHI of 8 is the highest score possible on the PISA Scale. Of all the thousands of respondents tested so far in North America, Africa, and the Caribbean, it is infrequent to find two people with the same PHI score. PHI scores are reported to three decimal places except when a PHI score is an integer (or a whole number).

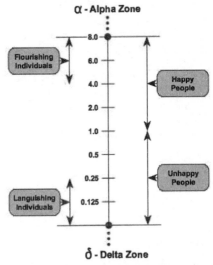

Personal Happiness Index

The Interpretation Key

Flourishing PHI > 4.0	Very Unhappy PHI < 0.5
Very Happy PHI > 2.0	Languishing PHI < 0.25
Happy PHI > 1.0	> means "greater than" ;
Unhappy PHI < 1.0	< means "less than"

The PISA Scale is a self-appraisal tool with several unique features that have successfully undone the flaws and limitations of the other tools currently used in measuring happiness. The following is the PISA Scale:

The PISA Scale [AKA: the Edo Questionnaire]

Instructions:

Please read each of the **twelve** statements below. On a scale of 1 to 8 (with 1 indicating not true at all and 8 indicating very true), circle the number that best represents your response to each statement. In other words, after reading each statement, circle 1 or 2 if the statement is **not true at all**, circle 3 or 4 if it is **somewhat true**, circle 5 or 6 if it is **true**, and circle 7 or 8 if it is **very true**.

Statements 1–6:

1. Generally speaking, I am an optimist.

 1 2 3 4 5 6 7 8
 Not true at all Very true

2. I do believe I have something to offer to others in this life.

 1 2 3 4 5 6 7 8
 Not true at all Very true

3. In case of an emergency, I have someone I can count on.

 1 2 3 4 5 6 7 8
 Not true at all Very true

4. When I need answers, I am usually successful in finding them.

 1 2 3 4 5 6 7 8
 Not true at all Very true

5. Considering the resources available to me, I am more fortunate than many.

 1 2 3 4 5 6 7 8
 Not true at all Very true

6. When I think about my relationship with God,* I feel reassured and less afraid.

1	2	3	4	5	6	7	8

Not true at all   Very true

This word, God, stands for Allah, Jehovah, Yahweh, or any omnipotent cosmic force or being.

Interpretation

Add up all the circled numbers and the total is your PISA Hope Score.

Statements 7–12:

7. I am currently under a lot of stress.

1	2	3	4	5	6	7	8

Not true at all   Very true

8. I do not get the respect that I deserve.

1	2	3	4	5	6	7	8

Not true at all   Very true

9. I have no trusted or intimate companion.

1	2	3	4	5	6	7	8

Not true at all   Very true

10. Lack of enough money is a constant worry of mine.

1	2	3	4	5	6	7	8

Not true at all   Very true

11. I have so many unanswered questions.

1	2	3	4	5	6	7	8

Not true at all   Very true

12. I am worried about my future.

1	2	3	4	5	6	7	8

Not true at all   Very true

Interpretation

Add up all the circled numbers and the total is your PISA Hunger Score. Since $\frac{HOPE}{HUNGER} = HAPPINESS$, your $\frac{HOPE\ SCORE}{HUNGER\ SCORE} = PHI$.

Calculate your PHI to three decimal places (or more).

Unique Features of the PISA Scale and PHI

Imagine a respondent—Individual A—who circled "8" in response to statements 1, 2, 3, 4, 5, and 6 and got the *highest hope score* of 48 and she circled "1" in response to statements 7, 8, 9, 10, 11, and 12—ending up with the *lowest hunger score* of 6. Her PHI will be 8.0 and she is therefore identified as a *flourishing* and contented individual. Next, imagine another respondent—Individual B—who circled "1" in response to statements 1, 2, 3, 4, 5, and 6 and got the *lowest hope score* of 6 but circled "8" in response to statements 7, 8, 9, 10, 11, and 12—ending up with the *highest hunger score* of 48 and therefore PHI of 0.125. He is a languishing individual. In between these two extreme PHI scores of 0.125 and 8.0 are countless possible PHI scores that span the entire happiness continuum, making the PISA Scale a perfect tool for monitoring the progress of a client or for ranking all the individuals in a cohort.

The PISA Scale does not ask any yes/no questions, does not require the respondents to rate themselves, or ask how "happy" or "satisfied" the respondents are with their lives. The PISA Scale measures the respondent's degree of hope and intensity of hunger. As shown below, one's level of hope and intensity of hunger reflect one's positive emotions and negative emotions respectively:

HOPE	VS.	HUNGER
When you are "hopeful," it means that you have a strong sense of impending good news or favorable outcomes.		When you are "hungry," it means that you have unfulfilled burning desires, feelings of severe deprivation, or insufficiencies.
Consequently, HOPE generates feelings of joy, anticipation, excitement, enthusiasm, interest, exhilaration, inspiration, and other positive emotions.		Consequently, HUNGER generates feelings of anxiety, fear, anger, annoyance, sadness, apathy, guilt, despair, and other negative emotions.
HOPE evokes positive emotions.		HUNGER evokes negative emotions.

PHI, the ratio of your hope score to your hunger score, is also the ratio of your positive emotions to your negative emotions. Those with higher PHI tend to experience positive emotions more frequently than those with lower PHI. As a result, PHI is an authentic measure of happiness.

The PISA Scale is a unique self-appraisal tool that does not require the respondent to do any judgmental self-rating or assessment. Instead, the respondents are simply asked to indicate how true or untrue are the statements made about them with no value judgments of themselves or critical comparisons to others. Consequently, social desirability bias is minimal to none.

The twelve statements on the PISA Scale are very carefully phrased to ensure universal applicability—across cohorts, cultures, socioeconomic strata, and ethnic boundaries. They are phrased carefully to measure what they are supposed to measure—hope or hunger—and also left wide open to capture a lot about the respondent. For example, when a respondent circles 8 in response to statements 1, 2, 3, 4, 5, and 6 on the PISA Scale, it tells us more than the fact that the respondent's hope score is 48. It also reveals to us qualitatively that:

- The respondent is optimistic about life, and she believes things are likely to turn out well at the end.
- The respondent has very high self-esteem with a strong belief in herself.
- The respondent has very robust human family support and there are people who care very much about her.
- The respondent has very little difficulty finding answers to questions that matter to her.
- The respondent is very thankful and grateful for the resources available to her, considers herself lucky, and has a good sense of resource adequacy and material sufficiency. She does not at all consider herself economically poor.
- The respondent is very spiritual, and she has a good and meaningful relationship with God.

Also true is that when a respondent circles 1 in response to statements 1, 2, 3, 4, 5, and 6 on the PISA Scale, it tells us much more than the fact that the respondent's hope score is 6. It instantly reveals to us that:

- The respondent is pessimistic in outlook and about life—with the belief that things are likely *not* to turn out well.
- The respondent has very low self-esteem or belief in himself.

- The respondent has no human family support and there is nobody who cares about him.
- The respondent has much difficulty in finding answers to questions that matter to him.
- The respondent has no reason to be thankful or grateful for the resources available to him. He does not see himself as lucky and has no sense of material adequacy or resource sufficiency. He considers himself economically poor.
- The respondent is not a spiritual person, and he has no meaningful relationship with God, Allah, or Yahweh. He is not religious.

Thus, the PISA Scale reveals important information about a respondent other than the respondent's hope score and hunger score—making the PISA Scale a tool for both qualitative and quantitative assessments.

The very valid concerns raised by Timothy Bond and Kevin Land (2019), in the *Journal of Political Economy,* about the inherent flaws of self-appraising one's own happiness are not applicable to the PISA Scale. Unique about the PISA Scale is that it does not ask respondents to rate their own happiness. The respondents are instead asked to comment on certain universally applicable facts of life, as the respondents experience them in their everyday lives. The word *happiness* is not even used in the PISA Scale, and social desirability bias is of no concern as the respondents are not asked to self-judge or compare themselves with others. Respondents are simply asked to comment on everyday life as they experience it—using a Likert scale of 1–8 to state what is true and how true it is. This feature of the PISA Scale is what differentiates it the most from all the other self-appraising happiness tools that are currently in use.

How Stable Is PHI?

The test-retest reliability of the PISA Scale is 0.95, and PHI scores are unsurprisingly very stable and reproducible. When you find your misplaced TV remote control or you lose the key to your car, there is no change in your PHI as neither is life-changing.

PHI stability seems to corroborate and affirm Diener's "set point" theory of happiness in which the late Dr. Edward Diener of the University of Illinois, nicknamed "Dr. Happiness," proposed that each of us has a relatively stable level of happiness or subjective well-being—despite life circumstances or external conditions. Additionally, the Hedonic Adaptation Theory of Diener, Lucas, and Scollon (2006) asserts that a change in set point may occur due to a significant life event—but only transiently. Accordingly, a change in PHI may transiently occur or a new PHI set point may result following any significant change in the level of hope or intensity of hunger.

The Three Types of People

As a result of the thousands of people so far tested using the PISA Scale, in the United States, Canada, Nigeria, Ghana, and the Caribbean communities, it is my conclusion that there are three types of people found in every community, nation, or country: **Zone A people** (who have high hope and low hunger), **Zone B people** (who have average hope and moderate hunger), and **Zone C people** (who have low hope and severe hunger)—as shown on the Happiness Index Map that follows. Zone A people have a PHI of 2.0 or greater, Zone C people have a PHI of less than 1.0 while Zone B people fall in between—with a PHI of greater than 1.0 but less than 2.0. Zone A people are more likely to flourish, and Zone C people are more likely to languish. By definition, to *flourish* is to live a happy life, in the highest range of human functioning; and to *languish* means to live an unhappy, hollow, and empty life.

The Happiness Index Map

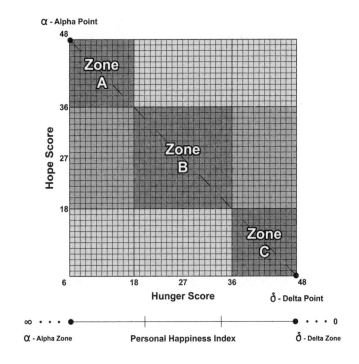

Personal Happiness Index

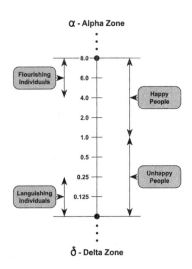

Based on the overall information presented in this chapter, the following five inferences are reasonable and logical to make:

1. There are happy people and unhappy people in every nation or human community.

2. The PISA Scale is a tool with universal applicability and could be used to measure and quantify happiness of individuals—across cultures, socioeconomic strata, ethnic, and national boundaries.

3. If one thousand randomly selected citizens of every nation were administered the PISA Scale, the happiest *country* should convincingly have the *highest* percentage of its citizens in Zone A and the *least* percentage in Zone C among all the nations.

4. The happiest person in the world should have the highest PHI.

5. Happiness coaches and advocates should concentrate on assisting their clients to do two things—boost their HOPE and mitigate their HUNGER, since $\frac{\text{HOPE}}{\text{HUNGER}} = \text{HAPPINESS}$.

To conclude this chapter, I would like to share a story, give some recommendations, and make an appeal.

The Authentic Well-Being Score

As all practicing physicians do, it is routine in my clinic that vital signs (pulse, body temperature, and blood pressure) of every patient must be taken and recorded in the chart before I get to see the patient—regardless of the reasons for the visit. Unique in my clinic is that the PHI of every patient is also required. When a vital sign is abnormal, the underlying reason must be determined and attended to as a priority. On one rainy day, as I was reviewing the chart of a nineteen-year-old patient, the vital signs were all normal except that her PHI was 0.127—the lowest I had ever seen. Just as I would have done in the case of a high fever or a very elevated blood pressure, I sent the patient to the nearest hospital emergency room for admission—with a handwritten note to the ER lead physician— explaining the need for admission and a psychiatric, or clinical psychology consult within twenty-four hours. Despite my handwritten note followed by a telephone call from me, the ER physician was not impressed given the very normal blood pressure of 116/72, pulse of 78, and temperature of 98.7. The physician sent the patient home against my advice, and she was given an appointment at the outpatient psychiatric clinic the next day. The patient, as I feared, did not show up for her appointment and all subsequent phone calls by my nurse and me to the troubled teenager were unanswered. We later learned that she had taken her own life—by overdosing on a bottle full of un-known pills. This poignant story made me a stronger advocate for routine determination of PHI—as the *authentic well-being score.*

Lesson Learned: An Expanded Definition of Vital Signs

The takeaway message from this tragic incident is that PHI (like pulse, blood pressure, and body temperature) is an important vital sign. And I concluded that routine determination of PHI is not a bad idea. As a physician, a certified happiness coach, a father, grandfa-ther, a spouse, an uncle, a friend, a colleague, and a good neighbor, the singular information I would like to have about anyone I love, is his or her Personal Happiness Index (PHI). With no desire to invade anyone's privacy, I would simply just want to know that my loved one's PHI is greater than 1.0. If it is not, *all is therefore not well.*

Recommendations

1. Wherever and whenever there is one available, the Chief Happiness Officers, or CHOs, should encourage routine determination of the PHI of every employee in the workplace and every student on the college campus.

2. Happiness coaches, counselors, nurses, doctors, and other clinicians should use PHI determinations in monitoring the progress of clients—after clinical or other professional interventions.

3. Positive psychologists and other researchers should consider the Edo Questionnaire as the universal and common tool for measuring happiness so results from different institutions can compare apples to apples rather than apples to oranges.

Currently, there are countless numbers of happiness scales, questionnaires, and inventories in use for ongoing happiness research projects, for shaping national policies, for assessing clinical progress, and for ranking countries, but none has the universal applicability across cultures, national boundaries, and economic strata as the Edo Questionnaire (or PISA Scale) does.

An Appeal

The singular appeal of this author is that the PISA Scale (aka the Edo Questionnaire) be seriously considered as the consensus questionnaire and the universal scale for measuring happiness or subjective well-being (SWB) because:

1. The PISA Scale is easy to administer, score, and interpret.

2. It directly and truly measures happiness—and *not* its correlates.

3. It is equally applicable to all individuals everywhere with very little or no concerns about social desirability biases.

4. PHI as the consensus unit of measure of human happiness will greatly improve the comparison of research results—worldwide.

5. The monitoring of progress in clients during clinical interventions will be possible and much simplified.

6. The country with the highest percentage of its (1000 randomly selected) citizens in Zone A and the least percentage in Zone C can *rightfully* be crowned the happiest country in the world.

7. The country with the lowest percentage of its (1000 randomly selected) citizens in Zone A and highest percentage in Zone C can *unquestionably* be regarded as the unhappiest country in the world.

8. Countries in between the happiest and the unhappiest countries are *similarly* ranked in the order of their percentage citizens in Zone A and Zone C.

This is very valid and the most logical as well as easy to implement—worldwide.

CHAPTER 12

HOW TO FIND, KEEP, AND LIVE A HAPPY LIFE

T he booming self-help industry offers an abundance of advice in the form of books, lectures, and social media posts containing positive psychology exercises that can purportedly make us happier. While well-intentioned, we can find this overwhelming, both in the amount of advice offered and the results. Perhaps you've attempted some of these happiness boosting activities that either did not work or failed to stick. Perhaps you are now frustrated because nothing has worked. It is also possible that you have been chasing after happiness in the wrong places as well as in the wrong ways, and now you don't even know how or where to start.

I wrote *The Happiness Formula* to help people understand, and fully comprehend, what happiness is and, more importantly, what a happy life is, and how to find it, keep it, and live it.

As you have seen in the chapters of this book, and particularly according to the Triple-H Equation, Hope is a *macro-determinant* (or a major determinant) of happiness and if you know or learn how to boost your hope, a happy life is not only predictable but also inevitable. Living a life of hope is the best way to become truly happier because a happy life is a life that is full of hope. "What about success?" you may ask. To answer that question, let me take a little detour and explain why success alone is not enough.

Many people assume that success will always lead to a happy life. Accordingly, it is a long-standing notion of parents and mentors that if a young person completes his or her high school education, graduates from college, finds a good job, gets married, and starts raising a family while continuing an upward climb on the career ladder, a happy and a fulfilling life will eventually ensue. While this supposition sounds reasonable, a more careful examination soon reveals that a happy life requires much more than a litany of successful accomplishments. Success merely connotes a satisfactory completion of a task, venture, or project; a successful life is merely a life marked by multiple achievements—as those around you can *objectively* affirm and applaud.

In contrast, happiness is a *subjective* feeling of satisfaction, and a happy life is your feeling of satisfaction about your life based on your own self-assessment—not what others see in you or think about you. Accordingly, *a successful life* is an appraisal that an observer can make about you, whereas *a happy life* is strictly a self-appraisal that only you can make about yourself. A successful and enviable man or woman can be very unhappy.

Founding CEO of the Bill and Melinda Gates Foundation Who Left for a Post in a Nonprofit Soup Kitchen

An eloquent illustration of when and why success does not equate to a happy life is the story of Patty Stonesifer, a successful and enviable achiever on a national scale who rose through the ranks in the technology industry and was named by *Time* magazine as one of the twenty-five most influential people in America back in 1996. She served as chair on several prestigious boards, including the Smithsonian Institution Board of Regents and the White House Council for Community Solutions. She was, for ten years, the cochair and founding CEO of the Bill and Melinda Gates Foundation in charge of a $38.7 billion endowment. She was by every measure a successful woman.

On April 1, 2013, she gave it all up and vacated her enviable corner office to become the head of Martha's Table, a nonprofit organization in Washington, DC, which serves and feeds the poor. Despite the litany of professional accomplishments, an enviable salary, and an apparently successful life, she realized the emptiness in her own life that had to be filled. She therefore embarked on a new mission of feeding the poor.

Award-Winning Chef Leaves Fine Dining Behind to Feed the Hungry and Homeless

Similarly, Narayanan Krishnan, one of the CNN Heroes of 2010 and a young man of enviable talent and success, seemed to have it all. He had accomplished his long-term dream of becoming a successful chef by working hard to complete a prestigious apprenticeship, studying under world-class mentors in the highly competitive field of cooking and catering. Eventually, he became an award-winning chef who was well paid working for a high-end five-star hotel group in India. Because of his natural talent, hard work, and acquired skills, he was placed on a short list for promotion to an elite job assignment in Switzerland.

He was already bound for Europe when he decided to make a quick trip to the Indian city of Madurai to visit family and bid them goodbye. It was on his way from a religious temple that he saw an old man eating his own human waste. Narayanan Krishnan was so struck with horror and pity that this singular experience awakened in him a personal spiritual compulsion to do something substantive about such a poignant human condition. Despite his prospect of becoming a top chef in Switzerland, Narayanan abandoned his overseas travel plans and instead decided to stay in India and use his profession as a chef to fulfill a larger mission of feeding the hungry and the homeless who live on the streets. Convinced of his new destiny, Mr. Krishnan smiled with joy when describing the gift of personal peace, satisfaction, and contentment that he has received as a result of his new mission.

During the CNN Heroes of 2010 Award broadcast, he said, "This is what I want to do for the rest of my life because there is a driving force, an inspiration, and a flame inside of me." Like Ms. Stonesifer, Mr. Krishnan felt the urge within and decided to follow the path that held the best promise for his personal fulfillment, sustained happiness, and true contentment.

Like Patty Stonesifer and Narayanan Krishnan, Sherry Lansing, in 2004, shocked the business world when she left her position as the head of Paramount Pictures to pursue philanthropy as a full-time engagement. She was the CEO of Paramount Pictures and formerly had been the president of production at the 20th Century Fox, the first woman to have headed a major film studio. She was involved in the production, marketing, and distribution of more than 200 films, including Academy Award Winners such as *Forest Gump, Braveheart,* and *Titanic.* Although she had become the enviable symbol of female empowerment as the first woman production chief at Fox and then CEO at Paramount, she did not feel fulfilled. As she left the motion picture industry where she was very successful and accomplished to help fight cancer and promote public education, she said the change was very exhilarating. As she put it, "I feel like I have a new life."

Many accomplished individuals have indeed switched from their highly successful endeavors to attend to other pressing hungers in their lives—in search of personal fulfillment. This switch from a successful endeavor to a totally different line of engagement is not always and exclusively driven by the desire to go philanthropic. For example, there are many highly decorated civil servants and accomplished politicians who quit their positions of tremendous success, influence, power, and authority in order to spend more time with family or, unapologetically, to make more money in the private sector. Not unusual are many celebrities in the field of music, theatrical arts, or sports, who later in life do go back to engage in intellectual pursuits despite their enviable success and current affluence. Also, there are well-known stories of very successful and accomplished Catholic priests who eventually denounce their vows of celibacy due to feelings of unfulfillment. In each of these cases, everyone is simply addressing the perceived void in his or her own life.

The common feature in all these stories is an apparent paradox: the lack of fulfillment amid success. This phenomenon of inner emptiness despite a successful life underscores the important difference between a successful life and a happy life.

A successful life does not necessarily mean a happy life. The former is full of accomplishments, whereas the latter is full of hope. For those who remain unfulfilled despite their many achievements, the recommended solution is to widen their dream and adopt a life of hope. I have observed that there are many, largely Zone B people, who are trying hard to find happiness but fall short largely because of their lack of awareness of the big picture and the role of human hope in overall life satisfaction. In those moments and instances when success is not enough, my specific advice to you is to probe deep into your own human core, find your consummate mission and your calling, and reach for hope. You can begin this process today by first determining your PISA score—if you have not already done so—to confirm what zone you occupy on the happiness index map. Then simply follow the instructions and recommendations provided in the rest of this chapter on how to advance to Zone A by living a life of hope.

Hope is that informed personal courage that energizes and motivates you to take the necessary actions needed to achieve a desired goal. It should not be confused with passive imagination or docile daydreaming with no follow-up action. Hope is the conviction that you will be able to fulfill your dreams. It is a belief, a feeling, a disposition, and an urge that calls you to action. It informs you, motivates you, and energizes you to execute. When your hope is high, your fears, your worries, and your doubts significantly diminish, resulting in a state of lessened psychic burden variously referred to as peace of mind, inner joy, happiness, or contentment—depending on the degree and duration of the experience. Hope is a form of a promissory note given to oneself in reassurance about the future. Hope radiates the willpower to dare and the spontaneous burst of energy for action. Hope is the feeling and the belief that tomorrow will be as good as or even better than today.

Where Does Hope Come From?

Although already addressed in Chapter 6, it is important to reiterate that there are five sources from which every human derives his or her hope:

- The first source of your hope is you yourself, personal virtues, and characteristic attributes such as your self-esteem, courage, and willpower—collectively called your *intrinsic assets*.
- The second source of hope is your family, friends, colleagues, and others around you who give you support, love, empathy, and understanding—collectively called your *human family assets*.
- The third source of hope is your own sense of material sufficiency and perceived adequacy of resources—collectively called your *economic assets*.
- The fourth source of hope is your personal intellect, education, experience, awareness, skills, and knowledge—collectively called your *educational assets*.
- The fifth source of hope is your own personal faith and ethos, prayerfulness, moral convictions, and religious beliefs—collectively called your *spiritual assets*.

These five essential human assets (real and potential) constitute the five sources of hope, and when you boost these assets, you consequently boost and enhance your hope.

How Can You Boost Your Essential Human Assets?

One proven way to generate or boost your own *intrinsic assets* is by seeking, finding, and holding on to a passionate life purpose, mission, or calling. Once you find the right mission or your true calling, your intrinsic assets proliferate and abound because the right mission or a true calling generates courage, willpower, enthusiasm, and self-esteem. A passionate life purpose or a calling is the best-known booster of intrinsic assets—and the basis of being in FLOW—that is, becoming involved in what you love and do best.

The principal way to accrue and boost your *human family assets* is by being thoughtful, by helping others, and by being considerate of everyone around you. In so doing, you are expanding your pool of well-wishers, strengthening family ties, and effectively widening the circle of your friends and colleagues through your own demonstration of goodwill toward others.

You can instantly enhance your *economic assets* by counting your own blessings and being thankful for what you have. Become the best steward you can be over your currently available resources. By simply valuing what you already have, what you already have appreciates in value. Above all, continue to actively and diligently find ways to market your ideas and skills. Work hard and try doing an honest job for honest pay, always.

Your *educational assets* are accrued and best enhanced by being open to innovative ideas, staying intellectually engaged, asking the right questions, and keeping informed, curious, and inquisitive. Recognize every opportunity as a chance to learn something new and remain eager to improve and sharpen your existing skills.

The best-known way to accrue and enhance your *spiritual assets* is by nurturing your own curiosity about the true nature of God and man, life and death, good and evil. Speculate about the purpose and the origin of human life and then act accordingly. Find ways to be relevant in the lives of others and be mindful of your intended legacy in life. Essentially, help write your own obituary by acting the way you wish to be forever remembered.

What Is a Life of Hope?

A life of hope is a particular lifestyle that is purposely fashioned and primarily adopted to boost all five essential human assets and consequently maximize one's hope. In actual practice, the first step is to identify a true passion of yours for pursuit as a life mission. During that pursuit, emphasis is placed on boosting all the five essential human assets—in thoughts, in words, and in actions. When you do this, you are living a life of hope.

Why Is a Life of Hope Important?

A happy life is essentially a life that is full of hope, and happiness has existential value. The Harvard Human Flourishing Program and other findings have shown that happy people live longer than unhappy people. They also have lower-than-average blood pressures; they mount a much stronger immune response and have fewer complaints of chest pains and headaches. Happy people never take their own lives because they are full of hope. People who are full of hope cope better and they also recover much sooner after any tragedy. A life of hope assures a happy and fulfilling life.

To begin and/or sustain a life of hope, here are seven specific steps or suggested changes recommended for you to make and follow:

Step 1. Choose hope over despair.

Step 2. Have a personal mission or life purpose.

Step 3. Widen your circle of well-wishers.

Step 4. Be a good and grateful steward.

Step 5. Exercise curiosity at all times.

Step 6. Cultivate your own brand of spirituality.

Step 7. Pause often and savor every moment.

Let's take a closer look at each of these seven steps and how to achieve them.

Step 1. Make a deliberate choice between hope and despair.

If you want to start a life of hope, the adventure must begin with a deliberate commitment to confront an important binary choice, the choice between *hope* and *despair*. Imagine that you have been walking along a one-lane road with no need to make any difficult choice, but your destination remains unknown. Then, suddenly you find yourself at a fork point where the single-lane road splits into two: pathway-A going west and pathway-B going east. Now you are faced with a difficult binary choice.

However, the choice before you (though binary) is *not* about taking pathway-A or pathway-B; rather, it's about *doing something*—anything—versus *doing nothing* (simply standing still without moving any further). The former represents *hope*, and the latter represents *despair*. Hope, in a whisper, invites you to keep on walking like the explorer and adventurer that you are. Hope does not insist or even suggest which path you should take. Hope simply urges you to dare enough to take a chance (any chance) and choose a path (any path) even though there are no guarantees. "No try, no gain, and you've got to play to win," hope whispers repeatedly into your right ear. "It is time to dream and step to the canvas on the easel in front of you and paint your own picture—any picture of your own future," hope pleads with you.

"Don't do it, don't do it," despair murmurs into your left ear. "Ignore the invitation to dare. Remain right where you are. Trying makes no difference because nothing really matters in the end. Today is just like yesterday and tomorrow will not be any different from today. Stay where you are and don't even bother to move any further!" says *despair*.

A Fork Point on the Road

A fork in the road generally does require a choice between taking pathway-A or pathway-B. Much more fundamentally, however, it demands that you choose between doing *something* versus doing *nothing*. It is primarily a choice between remaining stagnant, paralyzed by fear, doubt, and despair, and unable to move on further versus having the courage to dare to move on and take a chance with either pathway-A or pathway-B, full of hope that there could be light at the end of either tunnel.

Dear reader, I plead with you to listen to the whisper of *hope* and disregard the murmur of *despair*. Decide to move on and take any path with the strong belief that there is light at the end of the tunnel—regardless of whether you take pathway-A or pathway-B.

If you agree with this hopeful sentiment, make the decision right this minute to commit to an optimistic lifestyle. Do not hesitate or postpone your decision. After all, you are reading this book for a reason—most probably because you have a desire for a happier life.

It is not enough to merely wish to be happy. You must make a commitment to find happiness. Remember that an expressed wish remains a *mere* wish unless there is a *commitment* to implement and execute. It is only after commitment that a *wish* becomes a *goal*. The power of any commitment is even more potent when you formalize it in writing. I ask that you therefore consider signing or putting your initials at the bottom of the personal note of commitment displayed below. This makes it a binding contract with yourself. Symbolically it memorializes your commitment on this day to live a life of hope—a new way to live in pursuit of personal happiness and fulfillment. Please sign and date this commitment now, but *only* if it reflects your true and sincere feelings about the choice of hope over despair.

Personal Note of Commitment

I hereby make a commitment on this day to pursue a life of hope and optimism. By this choice, I have decided to make hope and happiness the major priorities of my life from now on. Weighing all the possible risks and benefits of my decision, I find that there is nothing to lose by choosing to live a life of hope. My choice is both genuine and deliberate, and my commitment is strong and without equivocation.

Signature_____Date_____

If you have signed, congratulations on taking the first practical step necessary to get you started on the adventure of living a life of hope.

Step 2. Identify your true passion and convert it into a mission and your life purpose.

Having an enthusiastic life purpose (or life mission) is an absolute requirement for a life of hope. A life mission should represent the core passion of your life and must spell out the *main* purpose of your very existence. When such a mission meets certain additional criteria, it is called a consummate mission. A consummate mission is very similar to the vision or mission statement of a corporation or the constitution of a nation. It articulates the essence of your life.

Your consummate mission must meet *five* criteria:

- First, it must originate out of your own personal interest and true passion.
- Second, it must address the hungers and preoccupations of others.
- Third, it must make good economic sense and be financially sustainable.
- Fourth, it must be challenging and intellectually engaging.
- Lastly, it should be wholesome and spiritually appealing.

Any vocation, avocation, special skill, or hobby of great interest to you can be molded or adapted to meet the above criteria and become your consummate mission. Once you identify the right mission, your willpower and other intrinsic assets instantly proliferate—suggesting that the often decried "lack of willpower" is in fact due to the absence of a passionate purpose or mission—rather than a true lack of willpower. In the core of every human being, there is an abundant amount of willpower, energy, and courage lying latent, waiting to be ignited by the right stimulus such as a meaningful life purpose. Living a life without a mission or purpose is like shooting arrows without any target.

If you need help finding your life purpose, your calling, or your consummate mission, a simple method called Creative AIMing is described in detail in Chapter 13.

Step 3. Expand your notion of family, broaden your circle of friends, and enlarge your pool of well-wishers.

An estimated 8 billion humans currently co-inhabit the Earth. They include your parents, siblings, and distant relatives; your neighbors next door; your colleagues at work; your business partners, clients, or customers; your servers at the restaurant you frequent; your mailman and delivery drivers; your supervisors and those whom you supervise; strangers at the mall; those standing in front and behind you on the line at the airport, at the post office, or at the zoo; the next seat passengers on the train, bus, or plane; people in the news who live in faraway places or speak in foreign tongues; the beggars on the streets; and the homeless people sleeping under the bridge. This entire universe of 8 billion people is available to you for consideration as part of your human family.

It is in your own best interest (if you want to live a life of hope) to expand your notion of family, to broaden your circle of friends, and to enlarge the pool of your well-wishers. You can start this process today by making it a habit to be considerate of others. Even through the simple act of greeting a stranger, you instantly increase the chance of gaining a new well-wisher into your expanding circle of friends and human family. The way to keep your human family expanding is by trying to increase your net pool of well-wishers at all times—by making friends, by simply acknowledging others, and by being relevant and helpful when you are around people, so you are missed when you are absent. Simply make everyone around you feel important and welcome. If you find it daunting and impossible to love *all* your neighbors as yourself, start by trying to at least love just one person—your spouse, a parent, a child, or a sibling—like yourself. The rest you should treat the way you would like to be treated.

When you are helpful to others in need, it gives you the moral courage and justification to expect that others will help you, and that gives you hope. Be mindful of every action you take and every word you utter to those around you. Do something every day to widen your circle of friends and strengthen the bonds between you and your well-wishers. Win a new friend each day or each week or each month to expand and grow your human family assets. Through your own thoughts and actions, you have 8 billion fellow human beings on planet Earth that you can potentially turn into your friends or your foes. Your true relevancy in life ultimately depends on how others see you as well as how you see yourself.

Step 4. Be a good steward, count your blessings, and value what you have.

No matter how poor you are, you are privileged with some number of basic resources at all times. You have a solely owned individual estate (no matter how small) over which you are in control as a steward. Whether the net worth of that estate is less than one dollar or more than one billion, good stewardship begins with a diligent appreciation of whatever you already have.

When you value and appreciate what you have, the value of what you have instantly appreciates. If you do not value what you already have, you are unlikely to be content with whatever more you get. The richest among us should not be determined solely based on the net worth in dollars. Though money is important, obsession with material possessions is a known obstacle to enduring happiness. He or she who has the least worry over money and material wealth is in fact the wealthiest among us.

Be a prudent steward who realizes that though one cannot live by bread alone, without bread, one cannot live at all. Prudent stewardship therefore means:

- Working hard and taking your employment seriously, always being punctual, and continuously fine-tuning your marketable skills or expertise;
- Looking for honest opportunities to buy low and sell high so you can make a reasonable profit;
- Being neither foolish with money nor enslaved by it;
- Counting your blessings and being thankful for whatever resources are available; and
- Appreciating what you have.

Step 5. Be curious, value knowledge, and learn something new each day.

Ignorance is the genuine original sin while knowledge remains man's greatest power. When a young child finally conquers that two-wheeled machine called a bicycle, both the joy of the teacher and the student are palpable but indescribable. Everyone who has experienced a true eureka moment remembers it for a long time. Knowledge is so vital for human survival that the newborn starts to learn immediately after birth without any prompting. Learning is not an option but spontaneous from the moment of birth. Even in later years, the two-year-old never stops asking the question why and the five-year-old seems never to have enough of bedtime stories. In adulthood, information continues to remain a premium commodity.

Most of us want to know the facts and the truth, particularly those facts and truths that provide answers to our important questions. Knowledge connects us all and enables us to share in the collective realities of our common human experience. As knowledge expands the human mind, it simultaneously tames the soul. Knowledge empowers and instills courage in us. It affirms self-esteem as well as self-confidence. Because hope is an informed courage, a life of hope is impossible without adequate knowledge.

Always exercise your curiosity by learning something new every day as a way of preparing for the uncertainties and surprises of life. For example, take every occasion as a learning opportunity, look up a new word in the dictionary, read about a country you have never visited, listen to documentaries on the radio or television, read a book, any book on any subject of your interest, read a magazine, any magazine of your choice, be informed about the national and local news of the day, seek answers to questions that pop into your head, find out how to in self-help books, and try always to know why. Often, simply knowing "why" has a way of lightening even the heaviest burdens in life by promoting hope. In fact, knowledge is power because it constitutes a major source of human hope.

Step 6. Cultivate strong personal ethos, have some notion of God, and formulate your own brand of spirituality.

In many cultures, there is a belief that a supernatural being, Spirit, or cosmic force (in one form or another) exists inside or outside each of us, acting as our guide, mentor, and guardian. This concept, though lacking solid scientific proof, has served humanity well by providing us with a feeling of having divine protection and supervision. Even as an atheist, you need something larger than yourself to believe in. At some point in life, many of us chose to embrace Christianity,

Islam, Judaism, or some other organized religious denominations based on personal experiences and the examples set by parents and mentors. Even those who subsequently or eventually come to scorn organized religion and detest formal rituals of worship do not necessarily all together reject the concept of spirituality. For many, and perhaps rightly so, spirituality is not about organized religion or any one specific set of religious doctrines. Spirituality is not even always about God. Spirituality relates to that attribute of our humanity that urges us to respond to the material needs of others. It is that mystical part of your humanity that urges you to do something positive even when it is not directly for your own apparent benefit. To be spiritual is to be your brother's keeper; not out of fear of ending up in hell but based on the love of others. Spirituality instructs you and helps you to realize that material possessions are only a fraction of what makes life worth living. Your spirituality enables you to develop strong humanistic ethos based on your notion of God, man, life, death, good, and evil. When your spirituality is complemented by a strong belief in God, it does strengthen your courage, dampen your fears, and enable you to find greater comfort and have more hope in life.

If you are seeking to live a life of hope but are very disappointed by the current cultural practices of organized religions, I advise you to adopt your own notion of God, cultivate a strong personal ethos or philosophy, and formulate your own brand of spirituality—by constantly asking yourself three questions: 1. Why am I here on Earth? 2. How long do I have? 3. Where am I going next? Nurturing your spiritual instincts and religious sensibilities is a requirement for a life of hope, but the quickest way to find spiritual fulfillment is by attending to the material needs of others.

Step 7. Pause to savor every moment, celebrate your achievements, enjoy the journey, and de-emphasize the destination.

Living a life of hope is a form of trying to live a balanced life. But a balanced life remains incompletely balanced unless it includes a periodic pause for savoring, reflecting, and making the needed adjustments. There are many who should actually be happy with their lives but surprisingly feel unfulfilled because they fail to pause, celebrate, and savor every moment. Not taking time to savor your achievements each day is like planting and sowing but forgetting to reap and harvest. As a result, you are constantly obsessed about the destination rather than the moment.

In addition to meditation, one practical way to pause and reflect is by engaging in some form of *regular physical exercise*. During a walk or while jogging, or during your time on a treadmill, is an ideal time to pause, savor, and reflect. Many of my best ideas have often suddenly emerged during physical exercise, when oxygen is flowing abundantly to the brain. Regular exercise is in fact a part and parcel of living a life of hope because exercise harmonizes the body, the mind, and the soul, literally and metaphorically.

In Recap: Commit to Optimism and . . .

If you want to begin a life of hope, you must first make a firm commitment to become an optimist rather than a pessimist. Next, find your true calling, life purpose, or consummate mission using the method of AIMing (described in Chapter 13). Once you meet these two prerequisites, you may then start to live a life of hope by observing the following simple daily routine:

- **Do something each day, no matter how small, to advance your chosen mission or calling.** For example, return a

business phone call, complete and mail an application, study
a manual, practice a speech, write a follow-up note, review a
written contract, do your homework, book a flight, register
for a license, attend a lecture, or do internet research related
to your mission or calling.

- **Do something each day, no matter how small, to put a
  smile on somebody's face.** For example, pay a compliment
  to your spouse; tip a waitress, the Uber driver, or the delivery
  man; visit a sick colleague, send someone a get-well note,
  or send a note for no particular reason other than to let the
  person know that you are thinking of him or her; give a ride
  to a neighbor; mail a present with a "I love you" note to your
  niece; allow the other driver to go first, give a surprise call to
  your uncle or aunt, acknowledge the doorman, offer a glass of
  water to your gardener, or send a thank-you card to your mail
  carrier.

- **Do something each day to learn something new.** For example, find the answer to a puzzle, look up a new word in
  the dictionary, read a magazine article, research a topic on
  the internet, read a self-help book, listen to a radio program,
  watch a TV documentary, or attend a presentation at the local
  library.

- **Do something each day to show your appreciation and
  good stewardship of the resources that you already have
  around you.** For example, make your bed in the morning,
  groom yourself, do your laundry, wash your car, clean your
  desk, cut your grass, pull the weeds, tidy your room, save elec-
  tricity, conserve water, and count your many blessings.

- **Do something each day to demonstrate or affirm your
  spiritual convictions, nurture your beliefs, and exercise**

some form of religious devotion. For example, perform any act of piety, honesty, or goodwill; say a prayer or grace before a meal; read a psalm; sing a song or chant; attend church, temple, or synagogue or simply make a sign of the cross; perform a ritual of your choice; play a religious song; play emotionally moving music; or take time to meditate on the questions: *What is the purpose of life?* or *Why am I here?*

- **Pause, reflect, and savor the day's achievements before going to bed each night —with a promise to yourself to do even better tomorrow.**

Every day, try your best not to skip any of these six steps. A consistent daily routine such as this will keep you on course to sustain a life of hope. As you carry out each of these steps, remain deliberate, and be mindful, thoughtful, and conscious of *what* you are doing and *why* you are doing it, so you will get the fullest benefits of your actions, rewards, and invigorating effects.

Performing these acts (or recommended routine) passively and absent-mindedly lessens their effects. For example, as you acknowledge the doorman with a hello and a handshake, remember and be aware that you are fulfilling (the doorman's) human hunger for inclusion and acknowledgment. As you leave a tip for the waiter, remember and be conscious of the fact that you are doing so to ease the waiter's own hunger for food and comfort.

Putting a Smile on My Wife's Face

On one certain day, I had not done my daily routine of putting a smile on somebody's face. As I was looking for something to do to please someone and show my good stewardship as well, I noticed that our kitchen sink was full of dirty dishes, glasses, and utensils. I pre-washed them, put them into the dishwasher, and wiped the sink clean. Unknown to me, my wife happened to be on the staircase—watching. When our eyes met after I had finished, she smiled broadly in appreciation, and I felt relevant and useful. It was that simple to put a smile on someone's face—in this case, my wife's.

How to Keep and Sustain a Life of Hope

Life is full of challenges for all of us. To successfully keep and continue to sustain a life of hope, you must develop the habit of responding thoughtfully rather than impulsively when confronted with the incidental challenges of daily life. You must always remember that the overall goal of living a life of hope calls for constant accrual and enhancement of the five essential human assets—intrinsic assets, human family assets, economic assets, educational assets, and spiritual assets. Learn to look at life through the lens of the Triple-H Equation:

$$\frac{HOPE}{HUNGER} = HAPPINESS$$

In other words, assess every situation that you confront based only on its impact on your *hopes* and your *hungers*. Any action, activity, or circumstance that does not enhance your assets or mitigate your hungers should be considered irrelevant. For example:

1. How should you respond when a discourteous driver cuts in front of you on your way to work during busy traffic?
2. What should you do when you face a false accusation in the workplace? Do you stay silent, just do your work, and keep to yourself or do you become indignant and pick a fight with everyone involved?
3. What should you do as a customer if you are dissatisfied with the service rendered at a department store or in a restaurant?

4. Where can you find the extra reservoir of energy to honor your obligations at home after a busy and exhausting day at work?

5. How should you deal with issues of your own mortality especially after attending the funeral service of a close colleague or family member? What should you take away from the eulogies and the tributes that you heard? How can you best use this and other sad occasions to improve your own life?

6. What is the best approach to finally attend to chores that have accumulated because of your inaction?

7. If inexplicably, you suddenly feel apathetic and somewhat in a stupor, what should you do to regain your focus on things that matter?

Situational challenges such as these are inevitable in everyday life and can become serious distractions and real impediments to the successful sustenance of a life of hope. Making the wrong decisions in these situations may lead to diversions that have the potential of interrupting the accrual of the five essential human assets from which human hope is derived.

Based on all that we now know, here are suggestions on how you may deal with these seven frequently encountered scenarios in everyday life. The suggestions offered illustrate how you should analyze arising incidents based on their impact on your essential human assets and your inborn hungers.

Situation 1: The Commuters' Traffic Scenario

You are commuting to or from work, and you have just stopped at a red traffic light. Not even one second after the light turns from red to green, the driver behind you beeps his horn angrily while screaming at you to move, accompanied by a profane finger gesture. As you finally proceed on your way at the legal speed limit, the same impatient driver or another driver of similar temperament cuts in front of you suddenly, causing you to slam on your brakes. He then speeds away, driving well above the speed limit as he continues to change from lane to lane.

How should you respond and what should you do, if anything at all, in order to stay on course and continue your life of hope unimpeded by incidental distractions such as this?

ANSWER:

Continue to carefully drive the rest of the way and just be grateful that all went well. Admittedly, an encounter with an inconsiderate and discourteous driver(s) is truly appalling and can be very upsetting; however, in the context of living a life of hope, the recommendation is to do nothing since your car is not damaged, you have suffered no physical injury, and your five essential human assets are not under threat. Aggressive drivers are often in a hurry according to the acuteness of their own hungers and/or their immediate priorities. They act without consideration for you and the other drivers on the road. Since this incident is of no consequence to your life of hope, just continue to drive safely. You must not allow an incident such as this to ruin your day or divert your attention away from your own priority, which is living a life of hope. In fact, you should be thankful because things could have been much worse. There are some people who have experienced something similar and who screamed back or retaliated out of impulse, resulting in a police officer's involvement in some instances. When and if you can analyze and respond accordingly as just advised, discourteous drivers will have very little effect on you and your day.

Situation 2: False Accusation Scenario

You have just returned to work after a two-week vacation only to find out that the colleague who had assumed your duties while you were away has been circulating rumors about you. He claims that he discovered you had been not only inefficient but negligent and the bad seeds he planted with others in your office have grown in your absence. First, what is at stake here? How should you respond, and what should you do, if anything at all, without deviating in any way from your ongoing commitment to live a life of hope?

ANSWER:

The workplace is an important contributor to your human family assets, and you cannot afford to do nothing about a hostile workplace if you intend to sustain a life of hope. Writing off the workplace without first making an honest effort to mend fences is like writing off your neighborhood or your extended family and denying yourself an important pool of potential well-wishers. Doing nothing in a case like this has the potential of creating a permanent source of distractions that is incompatible with a life of hope.

You are your own best friend and should never hesitate to be your own best advocate when it truly matters. What is at stake in this scenario is your good name, your record of stewardship, your economic assets, and your human family assets—all of which are important sources of hope. One good option is to deny the charges vehemently if they are indeed untrue. Do it without antagonizing anybody in the office and let your candor shine through in your denial. Confront the accusing colleague calmly and ask him to give you specific examples of your inefficiency and negligence. Rebut his claims and ask him not to do it again. Go to your boss or supervisor to complain about this falsehood and request an official denunciation of rumors such as this that disrupt cohesion in the workplace. By so doing, you are defending your good name, and possibly, you will win the empathy and sympathy of several colleagues.

Trying to live a life of hope does not mean that you should become passive, voiceless, and willing to roll over and play dead. Living a life of hope, in fact, requires that you actively seek to grow your human family, widen your circle of friends, increase your pool of potential well-wishers, and also protect your source of income—all of which are at stake in this scenario. Ask to be heard, and when the opportunity is given, address and expose the falsehood for what it is. Do not ignore false accusations because they pose a threat to your status and standing among your colleagues, who make up a significant fraction of your human family. All the while, take your job seriously, do your homework, improve your performance, and perfect your skills to empower yourself and convince those who harbor any doubts about your capability. In fact, as you engage in this line of self-defense, you are, in essence, showing the tenacity required for a life of hope. It is unhealthy to harbor your sorrows, ignore your pain, and continue to suffer in silence. You must reach for hope and do something to boost your *human family assets*—especially when they are under threat.

Situation 3: Dissatisfied Customer Scenario

During a transaction at a department store, the young sales associate seems to be impolite and somewhat dismissive of your requests and inquiries, treating you and your concerns not as seriously as you would like. She gives convoluted answers to your simple and very direct questions, and you feel that she is being unnecessarily difficult, too officious, or just simply incompetent. What exactly is at stake in this scenario, and what should you do about it?

ANSWER:

Since your priority is to live a life of hope, your focus should always be on how to boost your five sources of human hope, one of which is your *economic assets*. In this scenario, your economic assets are being threatened because your ability to maximize your buying power is being impeded by lack of support from the store's attendant, who seems somewhat indifferent to your interests. In order to live or sustain a life of hope, you must be a good and resourceful steward of your available resources. A part of being a good steward demands that you buy prudently and sell wisely, always making appropriate use of your buying power. This associate or attendant in question is unlikely to make this possible, and you should politely let her know how you feel about the service she is providing you. If there is no change in her demeanor, you can request another attendant, ask to speak with her supervisor, or simply walk away to go to another store.

Situation 4: Exhausting and Busy Day Scenario

You have just returned home after a long and particularly hard day at work. Instead of the relaxation and comfort that you were looking forward to enjoying, you get a message from your pastor reminding you of an emergency meeting of the health ministry committee scheduled for that evening. As you are physically exhausted on this day, what should you do, and from where do you get the extra energy to attend this meeting? And if you just cannot attend, should you feel guilty for not responding to this spiritually relevant invitation?

ANSWER:

Living a life of hope means that you have made the commitment to adopt a balanced lifestyle—which requires that you do something every day to boost each of your five essential human assets, namely your intrinsic assets, human family assets, economic assets, educational assets, and spiritual assets. An exhausting day at work has boosted your economic assets—one of the five assets you are required to boost each day in order to maintain a life of hope. You should rightly therefore perceive the call from the pastor as a chance to boost your spiritual assets—an important daily obligation equally relevant to your chosen lifestyle. From that point of view (or such a mindset), the motive to honor the pastor's invitation as well as the energy required to do so should instantly become available, despite your exhaustion—especially if you had not yet met your spiritual quota for that day. On the other hand, if you had already fulfilled another spiritual obligation on this day in question, failure to attend this one meeting tonight should not count as a serious violation of your commitment to live a life of hope. On such grounds, you should call the pastor and simply ask for an excused absence without any feeling of guilt—if indeed you are too tired to attend the meeting.

Situation 5: Funeral Service Scenario

A dear friend and colleague recently passed away suddenly following a brief illness. From all the tributes and eulogy paid to him, he seemed to have always done everything right. He was hardworking, successful, kind, generous, approachable, tolerant, understanding, religious, and prayerful. After the funeral service, you are confused about his untimely death in spite of an apparently clean lifestyle. You have therefore begun to experience an increased sense of personal vulnerability as you become concerned about your own mortality. What should you do to minimize your fear of death and feeling of vulnerability so you can continue to sustain a life of hope with greater courage and a lighter burden concerning the uncertainties of life?

ANSWER:

A heightened fear of death or dying is a normal and common human emotion, especially during or after the funeral of a close colleague, friend, or relative. The resulting thoughts of your own mortality also naturally arouse spiritual awareness, which makes it a perfect time to think about how to enhance your spiritual assets and rededicate yourself to a life of hope. Funerals give us a special chance to reflect on the important goals in our lives and to reaffirm the necessity of preparing for the inevitable the best way we can and as soon as we can. Take special note of the fact that issues of personal courage and character, service to those around us, stewardship and resourcefulness, knowledge and expertise, and faith and devotion to God are the recurrent themes in every eulogy. Also note that the deceased is mourned and remembered for how he or she *lived* and *hoped*. Eulogies during funerals should impress upon us that ultimately, a fulfilled life is that life that was spent bringing hope and peace to ourselves and to others.

Attending another person's funeral will always make you think about your own mortality. The thing to do is to use the opportunity to think and plan how you want to be remembered when you are gone. Even though a life of hope has several health advantages, including improved longevity, it does not grant immortality to anyone.

Situation 6: Procrastination Scenario

Inexplicably, you have recently found yourself putting off important chores and personal errands. You have e-mails awaiting replies, a package to be mailed to a colleague, housecleaning that needs to be done, phone calls to be made, defective merchandise that needs to be returned to the local store, a huge pile of dirty laundry,

a doctor's appointment that you need to schedule, and a legal document that needs to be notarized and mailed. What should you do to
break this cycle of inaction, so you continue to stay on course and
sustain a life of hope?

ANSWER:

One method I have used successfully to catch up with accumulated chores is to make a to-do list of all the things I need to do. I list
the easiest-to-achieve tasks first and the more difficult ones last. For
example, I begin the list with simple tasks such as brushing teeth,
washing face, making bed, or saying morning prayers, which I regularly and easily perform as part of my everyday routine. I put them
down on the to-do list anyway for the technique to work. Starting
in the morning from the top of the list, I perform the easier tasks
first—making my bed and saying my morning prayer. As I achieve
each task, I put a big check mark beside it, and then pause to savor
and enjoy the achievement just made. That sense of achievement
then motivates me to tackle the next task on my list because hope
begets hope, and each sense of accomplishment enhances the desire
to make further gains. Surprisingly, I soon transition from the easiest
tasks to the harder ones on the list, rather seamlessly.

I have taught this simple technique to several residents and
my medical students from whom I have received feedback full of
gratitude.

Try it any day and you will be surprised how well it works.

Situation 7: Apathy and Stupor Scenario

You wake up on a Saturday morning feeling uncharacteristically
lethargic, lazy, and fatigued—either because you did not sleep well or
despite a good night's rest. You are neither ill nor in distress but just

have a foggy feeling instead of your usual enthusiasm about another day of a wonderful life. What can you do to regain your usual self and continue to accrue the five essential human assets that you need in order to sustain a life of hope?

ANSWER:

Occasionally, a car may need a jump start and a computer may need to be rebooted. Similarly, the human body may occasionally need to recharge. When the above scenario happens to you, don't be alarmed. In fact, expect it but understand it as a call for a reboot. No matter how reluctantly or slowly it takes you, get engaged in some form of motion or any physical movement to shake off the fogginess. Nature seems to imply in various ways that there is something special about motion—in the form of a wave, stretch, vibration, flow, or rotation. In fact, one major difference between living things and nonliving things is the ability of a living thing to move and breathe. Moreover, locomotion—the ability to move from one place to another—is what fundamentally differentiates animals from plants. Even at the atomic level, the electrons are constantly in a vibratory motion in their respective shells. The Earth itself endlessly rotates on its axis as it simultaneously orbits the sun. Therefore, during mental boredom, fatigue, stupor, and stagnation, the therapy of motion (in the form of physical exercise) is the equivalent of a jump start, reboot, or recharge. Multiple studies have shown that physical exercise, especially when you do it regularly, improves both mental health and physical well-being. When you find yourself in a slump, muster energy to begin some form of movement in order to shake things up. One approach is to take three deep long breaths to allow an increase in the flow of oxygen to your brain. Stretch your legs, and then your arms as you take a yawn. Turn your head to the right until you are able to take a good look at the top of your right shoulder, and then to the left until you are able to see the top of your left shoulder. Flex your neck so that your chin is pressing tightly against your chest. Next, extend your neck until your chin is pointing straight at the ceiling. Repeat these movements one more time and then take a short slow walk around the room with your knee raised as high as possible during each step you take. Movements such as these are reviving enough to shake off your fogginess.

As you live a life of hope, you will occasionally fall off the wagon. What to do in such instances is to get up as quickly as you can and get back on board.

CHAPTER 13

CREATIVE AIMING—A SIMPLE WAY TO FIND YOUR LIFE MISSION

To make sure we are speaking the same language, let's review a few important terms:

- A *wish* is a desire that you are feeling or expressing.
- A *goal* is a wish that you have decided (or committed) to execute.
- A *mission* is a major goal or a set of important goals to which you are strongly dedicated.
- A *life mission* is a purpose or a goal to which you are willing to remain dedicated until death.
- A *consummate mission* is a perfect and wholesome mission that meets all your human needs.

- A *calling* is a perfect life purpose or that niche that seems naturally made just for you.

Potentially, each one of us is uniquely consequential to the entire human race; if only we can identify our true calling and unleash our capacity to hope and dream. Lamentably, there are many who live their entire lives without ever identifying their true calling. Consequently, they never become optimally accomplished or fulfilled. We all need a goal to pursue, otherwise we fall into despair or bad habits, or die of boredom. We need a mission to engage us and to motivate us, and a calling to give us the wings to fly and soar. It all begins with a wish.

A *life of hope* is a lifestyle that is designed primarily to maximize hope by constantly boosting the five essential human assets as one pursues a mission or calling. Thus, in order to successfully live a life of hope, you need *a passionate purpose* around which to build a life full of hope.

To "AIM" is to Adapt (or Adopt) an Interest of yours as a Mission. Through the process of AIMing, you can *creatively* mold, shape, and adapt a personal interest (a vocation or avocation) of yours until it satisfies the five necessary characteristics of a consummate mission. This is begun by making a comprehensive list of all the vocations and avocations that interest you, including your current occupation if applicable. Then thoroughly review your list to determine which one or two of the listed interests are most suitable for adoption as your mission—keeping in mind the five defining characteristics of an ideal or consummate mission.

For example, your consummate mission must

- Originate from a passionate (vocational or avocational) interest of yours;

- Be inclusive in scope and altruistic in nature;
- Be financially sustainable or make good economic sense;
- Be adequately challenging intellectually, technically, or artistically; and
- Have some spiritual or religious appeal and wholesome intentions.

Finding Your Mission or Calling—as a Student

If you are a college student and not sure what your mission or calling should be, try starting with your favorite academic subject or your college major. Take for example a story that aired on National Public Radio (NPR) on November 28, 2013, entitled "The Coolest Thing Ever: How a Robotic Arm Changed Four Lives." This story was told by science writer Joe Palca on *NPR Morning Edition*:

> Three engineering undergrads at Rice University gave a teenager with a rare genetic disease something he'd always wished for: the ability to turn off the light in his room. It may not seem like much, but for 17-year-old Dee Faught, it represents a new kind of independence.
>
> Dee can't operate a light switch because he can't reach far enough from his wheelchair. He has a disorder called osteogenesis imperfecta, also known as brittle bone disease. In addition to breaking easily, Dee's bones are tiny. His legs and arms are all twisted up.
>
> The three Rice students heard about Dee in an unusual freshman engineering class. Instead of learning engineering principles from a book, students form teams to come up with engineering solutions for real-world problems. The team's first step was to meet their client.
>
> "We walked through Shriner's Hospital for Children," says Nimish Mittal, one of the trio. "One of the nurses led

us to this patient room, and right smack dab there in the center was Dee sitting there in his wheelchair, with just a big smile on his face, waiting to see us."

"It was surprising seeing how small he was at 15 years old at the time," says Matthew Najoomi, the second member of the team. "I guess it was a little bit emotional when we first met him, because we felt bad for him being a teenager. We'd been through that phase. And on top of that, he has to deal with brittle bone disease. And we wanted to do as much as we could to relieve that."

At first, Mittal says, they were planning to build him something simple, like a reaching stick of some sort. "But when we met Dee, we were all really excited and we said, no, we need to go all out and do the best thing we could possibly do for him," he says.

So, the team decided to make a portable robotic arm that would attach to Dee's wheelchair so he could reach things all around him. At the end of the arm there would be some kind of gripper Dee could use to pick things up.

Rice has a well-equipped lab for engineering students called the Oshman Engineering Design Kitchen where the trio could work on the arm. The project didn't look that hard on paper, but when they actually started building the arm, "we hit a ton of roadblocks," says Sergio Gonzalez, the third member of the trio. "At the beginning we were working on what design we should use for the gripper. Like would it be like a scoop thing? Would it be sort of like this claw? Would it be three prongs? Would it be two prongs? Would it look exactly like a hand and have five digits and clamps around something?"

In the end they decided on something that looked like

a pair of pincers with flat paddles at the end. But there was just one problem: The gripper kept dropping things. And there was an even bigger problem. The arm wasn't nearly finished, but the engineering course was ending. But the team members say the idea of not finishing the project never entered their minds.

"We had someone who came and sat down in front of us, and asked for our help," says Najoomi. "We had to finish something for Dee," says Mittal. "We couldn't honestly leave this project because we would have left Dee hanging."

So, the class ended, and the team kept going. All the rest of their freshman year, through the summer and the next school year, the trio kept at it.

Finally, they cracked the gripper problems. "We changed the materials we used at the end," says Mittal. "We changed the angle at which it was touching the objects; we made it a little bit bigger so there's more contact with the objects that we were picking up."

At the end of September, two years after they first got the assignment, Najoomi, Gonzalez, and Mittal delivered a working model of the robotic arm to Dee.

When the team handed the arm controller to Dee, he got the hang of it right away.

"I picked up a towel," says Dee. "I picked up hats, and then I picked up a shirt. And I picked up stuff like a cup, an orange, and a book." Just normal stuff. Boring, really, but not for Dee. "It was actually the coolest thing ever."

No more will he have to ask for help to turn off the light in his room.

For the engineering undergrads, the project could have life-changing consequences, too.

"This has definitely refined the engineering I want to do," says Gonzalez. "Because it's an engineering focused on helping people."

Mittal agrees. "I definitely want to continue this kind of work throughout my life," he says.

"It's been a lot of sacrifice timewise on our end," says Najoomi. But "it pales in comparison to how rewarding it is to see him actually use [the arm] and smile."

In this story, two engineering students—Gonzalez and Mittal—decided to adopt their college major, which was engineering, not only as a career but as their life mission. According to Gonzalez, the experience he gained during the project, "refined the engineering," as he once knew it and elevated it to a new level. Right then and there, *creative* AIMing took place. Apparently, the altruistic nature of "an engineering focused on helping people" gave their interest in engineering an additional passionate boost, converting an engineering major from a mere future career into a calling that met all the five characteristics of a consummate mission.

- Engineering was an apparent passionate interest of Gonzalez and Mittal, and hence, they chose it as their major.
- Prosthetic design engineering is inclusive and altruistic since it will offer tangible assistance to others, especially people with disabilities.
- Engineering makes good economic sense, and it is financially sustainable since engineers generally make a good income.
- Engineering is intellectually stimulating and technically challenging.
- The branch of engineering that Gonzalez and Mittal have

chosen is spiritually appealing by virtue of its altruistic intent and overall wholesome considerations for the less fortunate.

This was how engineering students Gonzalez and Mittal found their true calling and life mission.

A Second Method for Finding Your Mission or Calling

If you are not a college student or a college major is not applicable in your situation, you can consider your current vocation or career (such as nursing, teaching, journalism, and so on) for possible adoption as a life mission. In fact, any occupation, vocation, or avocation including a favorite hobby or a passionate pastime can be considered for adoption as a life mission—as long as the required five criteria are met. Of course, not all personal interests of passion, all hobbies, vocations, and avocations are successfully adaptable into a mission or a calling. For example, unlawful, immoral, and inhumane interests or passions are not suitable or adaptable as a consummate mission since they cannot meet all the five criteria required of a consummate mission. They glaringly fall short of any wholesome, spiritual, or religious appeals. These interests and pursuits lack altruistic intent and are exclusive by nature. Also, those endeavors or jobs that you do because you must, but about which you are not passionate are unsuitable for adoption as a consummate mission.

A Third Method for Finding Your Mission or Calling

Even if you have no applicable college major and no current vocation or career to use as a starting point, you can start the creative AIMing process in the following ways:

- First, make an initial list of major vocations and avocations of interest to you based on your personal aspirations and passion. Expand and supplement this list by digging up everything you can think of about yourself, including your intellectual and entrepreneurial ventures of interest, your dream professions, favorite subjects in high school, job preferences, and political aspirations if any. Think of your talents and special gifts that others have previously noted about you and commended you for. Think of your favorite pastimes, your sports of passion, and any of your own creative works of art or literature that you have perhaps previously discarded or put aside and left unfinished. Also, consider any advocacy role that is of interest to you. Think of social justice, unfair human conditions, prevailing cultural practices, and social customs and trends that greatly offend your sensibilities and that you would like to eradicate by getting involved. Finally, review, edit, and condense the resulting list in order to eliminate repetitions.

- Next, take time to think about each item on the condensed list, line by line. As you ponder each item, vocation, or avocation on the list, try to picture yourself playing the role required or entailed. Imagine yourself experiencing the expected outcome of each possible career scenario and put a check mark beside each aspirational vocation or avocation that evokes great excitement in you.

- Consider each item on the list once again, but this time on the basis of whether the vocation or avocation envisioned can reasonably be expected, or possibly adapted, to provide relevant services and tangible benefits to others. If the answer is yes, put a check mark beside each such vocation or avocation.

- In the third round, consider each listed vocation or avocation on the basis of economic sustainability. In other words, does the vocation or avocation make good economic sense, does it have a plausible economic promise, or can it reasonably be expected to generate adequate income and livelihood? If the answer is yes, put a check mark beside every applicable vocational option.

- In the fourth round of vetting, decide whether each vocation or avocation under consideration is engaging and challenging enough as an intellectual, artistic, technical, or entrepreneurial venture. If the answer is yes, put check marks beside such options.

- In the fifth and final round of vetting, decide whether each vocation or avocation under consideration can be construed as ethically wholesome or spiritually and morally appealing. If the answer is yes, put a check mark beside such option.

- At this point, cross out all the vocations and avocations on the list, leaving only those with five check marks beside them. Among these, identify the vocation or avocation that appeals to you the most on the basis of personal passion; altruistic potential; economic considerations; intellectual, artistic, or technical appeal; and finally, on the basis of spiritual wholesomeness.

For example, the following AIMing worksheet resulted in the choice of a career in law enforcement by a twenty-six-year-old man whose aspiration was to become the chief of police, so he could change the culture of corruption that was prevailing in the county where he lived. As a basketball enthusiast, he also aspired to organize an exciting basketball league to keep teenagers in his community out of trouble after school and on weekends.

Vocations & Avocations	Vetting Rounds				
	Round 1	Round 2	Round 3	Round 4	Round 5
Practicing Attorney	✓	✓	✓		
Law Enforcement Officer	✓	✓	✓	✓	✓
First Responder	✓	✓	✓		
Military Service	✓	✓	✓	✓	
Basketball Coach	✓	✓	✓	✓	✓

As apparent in this example, the ultimate consummate mission that emerged—after five rounds of vetting—combined one vocation (law enforcement) and one hobby (basketball) into a consummate mission.

The end-point consummate mission should not be too rigid or static. It should remain dynamic and continuously evolving as long as the underlying passion persists and the altruistic, economic, spiritual, and intellectual appeals are preserved.

How Bill Gates Used Creative AIMing (Even Though He Didn't Call It by That Name)

Bill Gates, the founder and CEO of Microsoft, is an excellent example of someone who demonstrates how a passionate hobby could be adapted and molded into a calling through creative AIMing. Born in 1955, William Gates III showed great interest in computers from an early age. "There was just something neat about the machine," he declared to biographers much later in life. His parents, who had a law career in mind for him, became worried at some point that Bill's fascination with computers could become a distraction.

After high school, he got into Harvard but without a definite plan. Though he chose prelaw as a major, he also took mathematics and computer science courses. While at Harvard, he spent most of his time using the school's computers. In his own words, "It was hard to tear myself away from a machine at which I could unambiguously demonstrate success." After two years, and without graduating, he left Harvard and turned his hobby into a vocation by starting his own computer software company with his friend Steve Ballmer.

In 1980, Bill Gates created a computer operating system and became very rich. In 1985, he was declared the richest man in America and stayed so for eighteen years. Using a substantial part of this fortune, he and his then wife, Melinda, created a foundation that has become the most generous in the world for better global health, spending hundreds of millions of dollars on donated computers and life-saving vaccines and medicines. Gates adapted his hobby and vocational interest into a consummate mission. On the record, Gates has pledged to give 90 percent of his fortune away to worthy global causes before his death.

Indisputably, Bill Gates successfully found his life purpose through creative AIMing. First, he identified a childhood hobby of passion and great interest. He recognized it as his niche and adopted it as a goal to pursue. This goal evolved and became a life purpose. As a result, he found his true calling as a *computer guru* and a consummate mission that met all the five criteria emerged:

- It all began as a childhood hobby of *passionate interest.*
- It was intellectually *engaging and adequately challenging.*
- It was *inclusive* and potentially *useful to others.*
- It made *economic sense* and was *financially sustainable.*
- It ultimately turned out to be a *wholesome venture with spiritual implications,* appeals, and endorsements.

How Creative AIMing Influenced Morris Dee's Life

We can infer another example of how AIMing can unmask one's true calling from the biography of Morris Seligman Dees Jr., the cofounder of the Southern Poverty Law Center (SPLC) and, until March 2019, its chief trial lawyer. Morris was born to tenant farmers in 1936 in Shorter, Alabama. Despite these humble beginnings he grew up to be a resourceful and savvy businessman, even when he was in high school. He later attended the University of Alabama for his undergraduate and his law degrees.

During his undergraduate years, he witnessed the shocking treatment of Autherine Juanita Lucy, his classmate and the first African American to attend the University of Alabama, by angry crowds of white people spearheaded by the KKK, something that stayed with Morris for the rest of his life.

Savvy businessman that he was, he became a successful lawyer and the owner of a multimillion-dollar publishing venture. As he waited one day for a delayed flight at the airport, he read the autobiography of Clarence Darrow, which revived his repulsion for racial injustice and rekindled his interest in defending those who cannot defend themselves. This changed the direction of his career. In 1969, Morris sold Dee's Publishing Company for several million dollars. He later explained: "I had made up my mind. I would sell the company as soon as possible and specialize in civil rights law. All the things in my life that had brought me to that point, all the pulls and tugs of my conscience found a singular peace."

Thus, almost instantly, Dees adapted a passionate interest in a consummate life mission that eventually became his calling. Through the process of AIMing, he had found a life purpose that was altruistic, challenging, financially sustainable, and spiritually wholesome. From that point on, Dees began filing suits to fight racial discrimination, foster integration, and scare hate groups with bankruptcy and threatening court verdicts, in spite of the death threats he often received.

Regardless of the type of work you currently do, and no matter your interest or passion, AIMing can help unmask your true calling *and* set you free to become as consequential as you can be to your immediate community and/or the entirety of humanity.

President Jimmy Carter and His Calling

Once your calling is unveiled to you and you have had "a taste" of it, it becomes difficult to abandon or ignore, even after an unavoidable change in career, sudden unemployment, or retirement. The biography of Jimmy Carter best illustrates this point.

Jimmy Carter was born in 1924 in Plains, Georgia. He was the oldest of four children, served in the Navy, ran the family peanut farm, served as the 76th Governor of Georgia, and ultimately became the 39th President of the United States, from January 1977 until January 1981. He was well known for his strong religious faith.

Because of his strong faith, Jimmy Carter had a keen personal interest in equitable justice. Both in domestic and in international politics, he was a strong proponent of peace, fairness, and equity. He signed the Salt II treaty with Leonid Brezhnev in 1979; negotiated the peace accord between Egypt and Israel; remained an honest broker in the Israeli-Palestinian dispute; returned the Panama Canal Zone to the rightful owners; and eventually received the Nobel Peace Prize in 2002. After leaving office, Carter could not abandon his passionate interest in justice, peace, and global welfare. In fact, post presidency, he continued his calling by visiting many countries as an independent observer during elections. He actively participated in the Habitat for Humanity project of building not-for-profit afford-able homes in hundreds of communities all over the United States and seventy other countries. Despite serious health issues, he has re-mained a worldwide moral leader and a local Sunday school teacher.

The Power of Your True Calling

Although every calling is uniquely personal, all true callings share five universal features that help boost *intrinsic assets* and make a *life of hope* possible. Your true calling provides you:

1. A powerful long-lasting inoculation against boredom or fa-tigue and it causes your zest for life to continuously soar

2. An avalanche of self-esteem, willpower, courage, and perseverance

3. A steady stream of personal gratification and a daily source of aspirational joy

4. A personal niche and psychological oasis that makes it pos-sible to experience FLOW

5. A chance to fully express your humanity

Once you uncover your consummate mission, life purpose, or true calling, the next step is to get to work and start living a life of hope as already described in Chapter 12.

Each one of us is individually and uniquely gifted with an ex-ceptional talent in one or two areas of human endeavors—such as music, poetry, mathematics, carpentry, masonry, law, entertainment, engineering, business, parenting, oratory, surgery, sports, or jour-nalism. A successful discovery of one's natural talent, niche, or true calling (when combined with the capacity to hope) can make im-mense difference in the quality and scope of personal achievements and overall fulfillment in life.

Sadly, there are many who live their entire lives without ever identifying their true calling. Consequently, they never achieve their full potential and become optimally accomplished or fulfilled. I have often wondered what could have become of Wolfgang Amadeus Mozart and Dr. Marie Curie if their talents in music and science had never been unmasked. What other possible endeavor could they have pursued as successfully, and how accomplished or consequential to humanity would they have turned out to be under this alternative scenario?

Some of us seemingly do stumble on our true calling purely by chance and, as a result, become quite successful and accomplished in life. Such was the case with Daniel Gilbert, the now world-famous psychologist who, at the age of nineteen, was a high school dropout daydreaming about writing science fiction. When he attempted to enroll in a creative writing class at a community college, the class was already full, so he instead registered in the only available course, which happened to be psychology. There he found his passion and the opportunity to express his latent aptitude in the study of human behavior. He excelled and ultimately earned a doctorate degree in psychology at Princeton University, became a professor of psychology at Harvard, and wrote a bestseller on the subject of *happiness* with translations made available in over twenty languages due to popular demand. Among his other many laurels was the Phi Beta Kappa Award for excellence in teaching—all made possible as a result of the serendipitous discovery of his true niche.

Usually there is a provoking event that ignites the hidden talent or awakens a latent passion in many of us and ultimately causes us to soar, sometimes much farther than we ever dreamed. Commonly,

there are four possible situations or triggering events or incidental
catalysts, and these arise

1. As a result of a transformative relationship or encounter with
   an iconic personality;
2. Following a momentous spiritual inspiration or profound
   religious experience;
3. After a painful loss, severe deprivation, or tragic event; or
4. During an occasion of personal curiosity or solemn
   introspection.

Curiosity was the trigger in the case of Adam Steltzner, a young
man who had floundered around seemingly without any aim in
life. He was a wannabe hard rock star with pierced ears and a funny
haircut. His apparent priorities during high school were sex, drugs,
and rock 'n' roll. Even his own father believed Adam would never
amount to anything other than a ditch digger.

One night, while on his way home after playing bass guitar at a
club, Adam became fascinated after happening to observe the movements of the stars in the constellation Orion. Though at the time he
was a high school dropout who had earned the grade of F twice in the
same geometry class, he became somehow driven by personal curiosity to enroll in an elementary physics course at a community college with the intention of gaining some basic understanding about the
movements of stars in the sky. While attending that class, he suddenly
got hooked intellectually, found his true niche, and eventually ended
up with a doctoral degree in physics. He later became a top rocket sci-
entist and eventually the team leader of the NASA unit that designed,
built, and directed the unmanned space exploratory rover named *Curiosity*, which successfully landed on Mars on August 5, 2012.

As inspiring and enviable as are the stories of Daniel Gilbert, the psychology scholar, and Adam Steltzner, the NASA engineer, it is of course *not* advisable to leave one's personal fate and fulfillment in life entirely to chance by passively waiting until a sudden event or encounter or misfortune or tragedy jolts us into action on the right path. On the contrary, these stories reveal that each of us has a calling waiting to be unveiled so we can be set free to soar, if and when we also have the right dose of hope and the power to dream.

During my thirty-five years of research on human hope, including a thorough review of hundreds of biographies, I have consistently found that those who are full of hope and pursuing their personal passion are invariably the ones who ultimately achieve a sustained satisfaction and true contentment in life. I believe that when the human capacity to hope is combined with the pursuit of one's true calling, a life of fulfillment is not only predictable but inevitable. Accordingly, my sole recommendation to you if you want to achieve a truly gratifying and fulfilling life is to start with the discovery of your true calling—and follow up with the recommendations presented in Chapter 12.

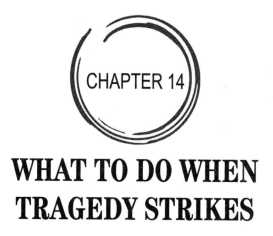

WHAT TO DO WHEN
TRAGEDY STRIKES

B y definition, a tragedy is an event that causes great suffering. Such an event is often sudden and usually unpredictable. One indisputable fact of life about everyday human experience is that no one is immune to incidental tragedies or misfortunes. What is equally true is that following any catastrophic experience, we as humans have the capacity to rebound and flourish despite (and sometimes even because of) tragedy.

Many tragedies are caused by natural disasters such as earthquakes, hurricanes, tornadoes, wildfires, flooding, severe droughts, epidemic infections, and large-scale environmental poisoning. Some tragedies result from human errors or the accidental failure of technology (as in the case of industrial accidents, airplane crashes, train derailments, and rocket launch malfunction), while other tragedies may be due to willful acts by individuals during the crimes of theft and homicide. Regardless of what kind of misfortune happens to have struck and under whatever circumstances, every misfortune or tragedy that we suffer in life impacts us ultimately through a common pathway—by intensifying one or more of our five inborn human hungers:

1. Hunger for food and comfort
2. Hunger for intimacy and trusted companionship
3. Hunger for answers and information
4. Hunger for inclusion and acknowledgment
5. Hunger for continuity and certainty

For example, when an earthquake or a tornado completely devastates the town where you live and work, when your spouse or sibling dies in a plane crash, when a terrorist bomb explodes and maims you, when you lose your home and all your belongings in a fire, or the doctor calls you to say that your biopsy is positive for cancer, the disruptive consequences of such events are not only economic but also psychological, spiritual, and social in nature with mounting fears, personal doubts, uncertainty, tests of faith, and the need for answers.

Without exception, the questions that instantly arise are: Why me? What have I done to deserve this? How and why did God allow this to happen? What do I do now? Will my life ever return to normal again? In every tragic scenario that one can imagine, the questions are basically the same. And my singular recommendation is that you look at life through the prism of the Triple-H Equation to find the ultimate recipe for sustainable happiness, which is *living a life of hope.* The fact is that regardless of the immediate cause of any tragedy—war, crime, accident, disease, or natural disaster—the resulting suffering and unhappiness is resolvable by increasing your hopes and mitigating your hungers. Consequently, those who know *how* to live a life of hope always have a better chance of withstanding and surviving any tragedy (big or small). While others may become overwhelmed with grief, anger, self-pity, and intensified inborn hungers following a misfortune, people who reach for hope (or who are already living a life of hope) rarely become severely despondent because they have the recipe for surviving, coping, and flourishing. Simply put, they know how to boost their intrinsic assets, human family assets, economic assets, educational assets, and spiritual assets—in order to maximize hope.

Five Practical Ways to Cope with Tragedies

Even as you grieve following a tragedy, the inescapable central question that awaits you is—what should you do now? My advice to you is to take five important steps that have been proven over and over to be very helpful. These five required steps or actions are (1) praying, (2) counting your blessings, (3) accepting what has happened, (4) adopting a new mission (through redemptive AIMing), and (5) forgiving those who have wronged you.

Using the diagram of a square (shown as follows) as your guide, mentally take a therapeutic journey within the square space. Make five imaginary stops, one at each of the four corners of the square and one at the center. During each stop, try to perform the recommended task indicated, so you can triumph over your recent tragedy as many before you have successfully done.

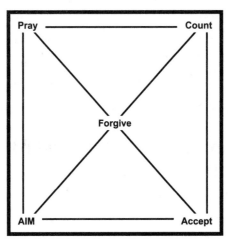

Post-Tragedy Therapeutic Square Space

Though all the five tasks are required of you while mentally inside the square, the exact sequence in which they are performed is left for you to decide since people grieve differently. My personal preference is to follow a Z pattern by starting with prayers and ending with acceptance in a Z-shaped sequence. Thus, my recommended sequence (or the Z Pathway) is to pray first and then transition to counting your blessings, followed by the acts of forgiveness, AIMing, and finally, acceptance.

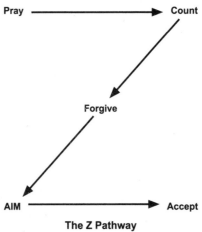

The Z Pathway

The Z Pathway traces my recommended route and preferred sequence for performing the five specific tasks required during the mental journey within the therapeutic square—starting with prayers and ending with acceptance. In essence, it is an intensified and most effective way to reach for hope.

How to Pray After a Tragedy (and Why?)

For those who have strong faith (or a passionate belief in something bigger and mightier than themselves), praying is the first line of response and defense when a tragedy strikes. A prayer is simply a conversation with God—a spirit, a supernatural being, or a cosmic force—during which you can pour out your thoughts, ask questions, describe your plight, and make your needs known in tears (if you like), in anger, loudly, or in a whisper.

There is no one special way to pray, nor is there a special language or format. Do it in your own words and in your own way—alone or with other members of your family—as long as you want and as frequently as desired. You can do it privately or publicly, anywhere and at any time. What to pray for includes strength, courage, and the wisdom to help you survive the tragedy that has struck. Prayer is the right medium and most accessible way to express your sorrow and simultaneously ask for help. It is a time to revive, nourish, and take advantage of your relationship with something bigger and mightier than yourself.

As you pray, state your case either calmly or emotionally. Make your demands in tears or with dry eyes. Also, pause and listen to hear God's reply because there are many who give credible testimonials about actually hearing back from God. For those who have strong belief in God, kneeling to pray is a frequent ritual. During personal difficulties or challenging moments, praying offers instant access to ask probing questions, renew a pact with God, confess, repent, and apologize for your past indiscretions. Just as parents want their children to ask questions and request help when necessary, so does God (according to the Bible). He wants you to come to Him with your thoughts and needs. Even for the nonreligious, prayers, affirmations, and rituals often become their instantaneous tool for venting when they are suddenly confronted by a painful loss or tragedy.

My Carefree Cousin Who Faced an Unthinkable Tragedy

My cousin Gloria, with whom I grew up, was a beautiful young lady and the only child of her very protective father, who became a widower following Gloria's mother's death during childbirth. Gloria always had everything she needed or wanted as a child, during and throughout her teenage years and early adulthood. She became married to a carefully vetted young army officer with whom she had several children. Gloria was never known to be religious or even spiritually oriented. During a brief separation from her husband, she had custody of her three teenage children and lived in a rented apartment. While on a brief business/pleasure trip to Europe with some friends, her three children died in a tragic fire that swept through their apartment. Upon returning from Europe and hearing the devastating news, she recalled, "I did not know what to do and where to start. I helplessly fell on my knees to pray for strength and direction. That was what I did and could only do and have done ever since." Today, because of how prayers helped her survive her painful tragedy, the onetime carefree, nonreligious Gloria now runs a self-styled "team of prayer warriors" with a full-time mission of praying, teaching, and coaching other victims of tragic circumstances on how to overcome their seemingly irrecoverable loss.

In addition to prayers, reciting certain religious affirmations and performing some simple religious rituals (such as making the sign of the cross) have been known to give instant anxiety relief by boosting one's courage and fostering a quick resolve. The most soothing of all prayers and the best reassuring affirmations ever may be found in the Bible, Koran, Talmud, and other holy texts or publications that address issues of loss and bereavement. Particularly comforting to many Catholics and other Christians are the affirmations contained in Psalm 23, which begins with "The lord is my shepherd, I shall not want." Also, prayers such as the one often attributed to Saint Francis of Assisi—which asks for courage and serenity to change the things that can be changed, accept those that cannot be changed, and the wisdom to know the difference—is a universal sentiment in all major religions. Skeptics who ridicule prayers often question why God, if all-knowing, requires verbalized reminders—in the form of prayers—before intervening on behalf of the faithful. For this reason, strong believers usually pray that the will of God always be done and in the manner of divine choice—making the acceptance of any tragic incident much easier. For many people, religion or spirituality is a default survival tool and the story of Gloria illustrates how easily even nonbelievers readily seek divine assistance in times of tragedy.

Counting Your Blessings After a Tragedy

Regardless of how severe a tragic incident is, the fact that things could have been much worse becomes apparent—almost in every case—soon after the initial shock. With the right mindset, there is always a reason to be thankful for the abundant privileges and advantages one continues to enjoy despite a tragic experience. This act of recognizing how much worse things could have been and taking stock of what advantages you do have—even while facing difficult personal challenges—is known as counting one's blessings. Such a simple appreciation of the positives, even as you mourn the negatives, is a potent coping strategy that can help diminish the pain and sorrow arising from a tragic misfortune.

For example, just recently, I tried to console a younger physician colleague upon hearing of the death of his father, whom I knew he loved very much. The colleague thanked me for my condolence and added, "My father lived a good life. And he has left behind a loving and closely knit family, several highly productive children and promising grandchildren, as well as a well-endowed foundation to help the children in the neighborhood where he lived and worked." With such a persuasive count of blessings, I had no doubt that my colleague had accepted the loss of his father and had moved on. Counting your blessings is an expression of gratitude for what you still have despite the loss.

Counting the blessings enjoyed in the past also worked for Nancy Yucius of Avon, Massachusetts, and it gave her the attitude that protected her from despondency as she battled colon cancer. Nancy had lived her life to the fullest without leaving any room for later regrets. She traveled; she ventured, laughed, read, and played with her grandchildren. When she was faced with the diagnosis of colon cancer later in life, her recounting of her many blessings and all the cherished wonderful moments in her memory helped her cope quite admirably. She wrote:

> Living my life so I'd have no regrets was a lesson I took
> in and believed in. I saved dimes and quarters while paying

my way through college to save for my own three-month tour of Europe. I've gone up in a hot-air balloon, traveled extensively, worked for good causes in my church and taught hundreds of children to read during my twenty-three-plus-year career as a special education teacher for Massachusetts public schools. My husband, David, and I raised three happy, productive children, all married now, and we have eight wonderful grandchildren. I've been lucky enough to have had a supportive husband who has allowed me to live my life as I wanted to live it. He did double duty around the house when I went back to school to get my master's degree, watched nervously as I took a ride on a Harley and silently cringed when I insisted on going parasailing. He wished me bon voyage several times as I traveled far and wide during summers when he had to work.

About her colon cancer, Nancy never worried much. She continued to count her blessings and relive the past triumphs and success stories in her life. Remembering the good fights and hard-won battles of yesterday and the belief that no matter how bad things might be, they could even be much worse, and therefore thankful—can be very therapeutic after any tragedy.

I once had a patient for whom I had delivered two of her three children. Subsequently, as a result of a tragic automobile accident, she became paraplegic. Just two days after the devastating prognosis of never being able to walk again was confirmed by the neurologist, she reportedly said, "I am so thankful that I am not only alive but still have the use of my two hands to hug my children." Hers is a profound statement that explains how to count one's blessings, and why.

Of all the positive emotions studied in the field of positive psychology, gratitude has perhaps received the most attention. Grateful people have been shown to have greater positive emotion, a greater sense of belonging, and lower incidence of depression and stress—as Pollak and McCullough (2006) and Madhuleena, Chowdhury, and William Smith (2023) have shown.

Why and How to Forgive

Kim Phuc was a little girl in Vietnam during the time of her country's conflict with the United States. She was first introduced to the world through a horrifying picture of her, screaming and running naked in the street after she was set on fire by a napalm bomb that was dropped on her village in South Vietnam. She now lives in Toronto, Canada, and her story of forgiveness is instructive in many ways.

In reaction to both the psychological and physical scars she suffered from that traumatic event, Kim became very bitter and angry with life, with America, and with all uninjured people, for years. At one point, she even contemplated suicide. She attempted redemptive AIMing and wanted to become a physician but did not have enough support in Vietnam. In 1992, she sought and got political asylum in Canada, where she now lives. She read and she prayed, and finally, through the power of forgiveness, she gained inner peace.

She wrote:

> It was a difficult time for me when I went home from the hospital. Our house was destroyed, we lost everything, and we just survived day-by-day. Although I suffered from pain, itching, and headaches all the time, the long hospital stay made me dream of becoming a doctor. But my studies were cut short by the local government. They wanted me

as a symbol of the state. I could not go to school anymore. The anger inside me was like hatred as high as a mountain. I hated my life. I hated all people who were normal looking because I was not normal. I really wanted to die, many times. I spent my daytime in the library reading a lot of religious books to find a purpose for my life. One of the books that I read was the Holy Bible. On Christmas Day 1982, I accepted Jesus Christ as my personal savior. It was an amazing turning point in my life. God helped me to learn to forgive, the most difficult of all lessons. It didn't happen in a day, and it wasn't easy. But I finally got it. Forgiveness made me free from hatred. I still have many scars on my body and severe pain most days, but my heart is cleansed.

While forgiveness of any kind (no matter how belated) is ultimately in the best interest of the victim, and often spiritually motivated as Kim had demonstrated, one particular form of forgiveness—agapeic forgiveness—is the most gracious and exemplary form that leaves no residual resentment toward the wrongdoer or anyone else. Though not by any means effortless, it is surprisingly the easiest form of forgiveness to execute because it is based on the knowledge, appreciation, and understanding of the universal inborn human hungers that we all share, from which all human urges and compulsions flow. It is a forgiveness based on a strong belief in the unity of all people and the conviction that we all as humans are afflicted by inborn compulsions with similar propensities for transgressions. In other words, "Except for the grace of God, there go all of us."

The priority in agapeic forgiveness is to give healing for both the victim and the transgressor since the only difference between them is the circumstances of life over which neither has absolute control. This was the rationale of Ronald Cotton of Winston-Salem, North Carolina, who spent eleven years in prison for a rape he never committed. He was wrongly picked out in a lineup of suspects by Jennifer Thompson (the alleged rape victim) in 1984. It was only after eleven years in jail that his innocence was finally proven. The remarkable thing was that during his time in prison, he harbored no ill feelings toward the accuser, the wardens, or the prosecutor. He was a model prisoner who, by all accounts, lived *a life of hope* for those eleven years.

Following his release by means of DNA evidence, he established a friendship with his accuser, saying, "Forgiving Jennifer for picking me out of that lineup as her rapist took little time. She was also a victim and was hurting. But I was hurting, too. I missed my family, my girlfriend and my freedom. But I knew who I was, and I was not that monster. Letting go of my anger so I can stay free in my heart was a choice only I could make."

As it turned out, the healing from the agapeic forgiveness that Ron initiated was quite infectious—as evident in this statement by Jennifer, who wrote:

> When I asked Ron if he could ever forgive me, with all the mercy in the world he took my hands and with tears in his eyes, he told me he had forgiven me a long time ago. At that moment I began to heal. Ronald taught me how to let go of all that pain. His forgiveness set me free that night. Without Ronald, I would still be shackled to that moment in time, and it would own me forever. I soon discovered that I could even forgive the man who had raped me [wherever he is today], not because he has asked me to,

nor because he deserved it, but because I did not want to
be a prisoner of my own hatred.

The outcomes for both Ron and Jennifer were that both became
healed through forgiveness but not exactly for the same reasons.
What differentiates agapeic forgiveness from all other forms of forgiveness is that it is purely voluntary, unforced, and timely executed
because of a preexisting readiness to forgive—in the fashion of the
late Dr. Martin Luther King Jr., who, while being flogged with clubs,
bitten by police dogs, and struggling to stay erect under the pressure of water from the fire hose, observed and preached forgiveness.
Dr. King said he had derived that kind of forgiveness from *agape*, an
understanding and redemptive goodwill toward everyone—as evident in the Platonic dialogues.

Redemptive AIMing

Following a tragedy, the pain suffered may leave a personal void,
uncover an unacceptable human condition, or highlight an existing
societal flaw that demands immediate attention. As a result, the need
for *redemptive* AIMing may arise. In creative AIMing, you adapt or
adopt a vocation or a hobby as a life mission whereas in redemptive
AIMing you adapt a painful incident into a preventive/redeeming
mission. In the former, you are searching for your natural calling but
in the latter, you are trying to redeem a social condition or a flaw. Redemptive AIMing is born out of a catastrophic event or experience.

The following are some examples of redemptive AIMing:

Candy Lightner: The Founder of MADD

Perhaps one of the most famous examples of all the people who
have executed *redemptive* AIMing is Candace Lynne Lightner, the

founder of Mothers Against Drunk Driving (or MADD). On May 3, 1980, Candy Lightner's thirteen-year-old daughter, Cari, was struck from behind by a car while walking in her residential neighborhood of Fair Oaks, California. She was killed, and the drunk driver drove away from the scene of the accident. The driver was a repeat DWI offender who had been released on bail for another hit-and-run drunk driving crash only two days before he killed Cari. It was his fifth offense in four years.

At the time, in 1980, although it's hard to imagine today, drunk driving was not considered a serious crime. In fact, alcohol intoxication was an accepted excuse for many otherwise unacceptable behaviors, including drunk driving. Immediately after Cari's funeral, Candy Lightner started a group known as MADD in her den on May 7, 1980. The purpose of the organization was to raise public awareness of the serious nature of drunk driving. She fought to promote legislation against the crime, first in California and subsequently nationally. She was particularly mad about the fact that the drunk driver who killed her daughter had been caught but he was probably not going to receive any jail or prison time for her daughter's death because of the public and legal sentiments at the time. In the depth of her grief during bereavement, she did something redemptive by adapting the painful incident into a mission that awakened the nation and the world to the now much-derided crime of drunk driving.

Through redemptive AIMing, the anger stage of Candy's grief was shortened as she got busy memorializing her daughter, Cari. As she later wrote, "I promised myself on the day of Cari's death that I would fight to make this needless homicide count for something positive in the years ahead." She founded *Mothers Against Drunk Driving* (MADD). She did not allow her anger to be turned inward into self-harm in the form of depression or suicide.

Wanda Butts and the Josh Project

Another example of redemptive AIMing is the story of Wanda Butts of Toledo, Ohio, whose son, Josh, accidentally drowned on August 6, 2006, because he did not know how to swim. In her grief, she channeled her energy productively to form the Josh Project, which raises funds to give free swimming lessons to children (particularly inner-city disadvantaged children) who could otherwise not afford it due to lack of access to swimming pools. She began the project locally in her city, and it gradually evolved into a statewide and national advocacy group for affordable swimming lessons. She began the Josh Project with just four students—herself, her daughter, and her two grandsons. For those first four students, learning to swim facilitated the family's healing and helped to abbreviate the anger stage of the grief process (which is potentially most destructive). This activity lessened the guilt, sorrow, and pain associated with her loss.

Wanda Butts has since made swimmers out of thousands of children nationally by adapting a personally painful incident into a mission to fill a perceived void, redeem an unacceptable social condition, or make improvements to a human circumstance instead of wallowing in grief or in self-pity. When tragedy strikes, many Zone A people use the occasion to make lemonade out of the lemons tossed at them.

As with creative AIMing, redemptive AIMing can provide a lifelong mission or a purpose around which you can build and sustain a life of hope and happiness. There are recorded accounts of successful and fulfilling redemptive AIMing stories where a victim looks back after several years to his or her life-altering tragic event and comes to regard it as a "blessing in disguise." People sometimes even come to refer to a tragedy as "the best thing that ever happened" to them.

Acceptance

Acceptance and a personal resolve to move on (following a tragedy or misfortune) is the final stage of the Z Pathway during the journey inside the therapeutic square. Like the other four tasks already accomplished on the Z Pathway, your arrival at this final stage is highly individualized because everyone is different, and the types of tragedies vary. It is a common finding that acceptance usually does not happen suddenly but rather takes place slowly over time. In fact, *acceptance* starts to build even as you pray for strength and courage at stage 1; gratefully count your blessings at stage 2; wholeheartedly forgive at stage 3; and find a new life purpose through redemptive AIMing at stage 4. During the different stages of the Z Pathway, the inborn hungers that were intensified by the tragedy are addressed and slowly mitigated one by one. Of all the five inborn hungers, the hunger for continuity and certainty often proves to be the most intense and also most difficult to mitigate. Acceptance, in some cases, entails contrition and deathbed confessions—on the part of a bedridden and slowly dying victim of a tragedy. In such cases, the problem of coping with death complicates recovery and acceptance.

Deathbed confession is a major way of coping or reducing stress during an impending death, and contrition is another. Contrition may take the form of repudiation of a previously held position, like the rejection of atheistic views by a dying atheist, or simply done by revealing previously held secrets.

These are called acts of *terminal courage and deliberate surrender* (TCDS), and they arise from profound introspection for reasons of self-redemption and can be a way of mitigating one's stress load in the final hours of life.

About TCDS

TCDS is an extreme option recommended in the case of impending death due to terminal illness or other situations when one only has a limited time to live. It is a method of coping and acceptance—a way of eliminating the earthly burdens of all forms of pretexts and misrepresentations in preference for absolute candor, confessions, apologies, reconciliatory gestures, solemn contrition, and repudiation of previously held positions such as racism and atheism. Remarkably, TCDS involves revealing personal secrets, disclosing previously closely guarded information, and sometimes life-altering announcements and pronouncements to surviving family members in order to heal and lighten the burden on the heart as one prepares for that irrevocable journey to the unknown.

The soothing advantage of TCDS was reportedly very helpful to the opera singer Luciano Pavarotti in his last days before he died of cancer in 2007. Other examples of deathbed redemptive confessions include those of Hollywood actor David Niven to his autobiographer; Israeli songwriter Naomi Schemer's confession about plagiarizing the melody of an old lullaby, something she denied vehemently until a few days before dying of cancer in 2004; and Geraldine Kelley's confession (to her daughter) of the killing of her husband, John Kelley, only after she was diagnosed with breast cancer, giving details—including where to find the body—just before she died.

Tor Hepso's Deathbed Confession

The most redemptive deathbed confession is one made not merely to get something off the chest but to also spread peace, renounce hate or violence, and restore justice or exonerate the innocent. Such was the confession made by Tor Hepso, who told his nurses about the murder of two women in Norway that he had committed in 1976 for which Fritz Moen, an innocent mentally challenged young man, was tried, found guilty, and put in jail for eighteen years. Moen was released after the deathbed confession of Mr. Hepso.

The uniqueness of TCDS is best illustrated in the reported deathbed confession by James Washington, a prisoner in Tennessee who suffered a heart attack, thought he was dying, and confessed to his warden about an unsolved murder he had committed. Unfortunately—or fortunately—he survived the heart attack. He was later charged with the murder to which he had confessed when he believed himself to be at death's door, but Mr. Washington then tried to deny his confession, apparently because his need for TCDS was no longer there.

How Mrs. Elizabeth Edwards Did It

In closing, let me briefly touch on the well-known story of the late Elizabeth Edwards to help illustrate how one can use the Z Pathway to cope practically:

Elizabeth's personal tragedy was that she was dying of metastatic breast cancer while also dealing with a well-publicized, humiliating, and heart-wrenching story of infidelity on the part of her politician husband, John Edwards. She had campaigned faithfully for him despite her physical incapacitation resulting from breast cancer, its treatments, and side effects. She *prayed* and *counted her blessings* as evident in her own words when she wrote, "In the simple act of living with hope, and in the daily effort to have a positive impact in the world, the days I do have are made all the more meaningful and precious. And for that, I am grateful."

She also *forgave* her unfaithful husband, John Edwards, allowing him at her bedside even in her final hours, as well as also buying a gift for the out-of-wedlock child from her husband's infidelity. She used redemptive AIMing by making a mission out of her own painful life incidents in speaking out publicly and writing a bestseller to eloquently educate others about her breast cancer. Finally, on her deathbed, she resorted to TCDS by describing her feelings and emotions, including her intimate instructions to her surviving children. What a remarkable woman and admirable journey on the Z Pathway.

Underlying each of these five methods of responding to a painful loss or personal tragedy is the universal human need to reach for hope—especially when there is a challenge or threat to life. The natural grief process itself is an example of the primal tendency of humans to reach for hope. You can use these methods of coping separately or in combination. All the five steps may not equally or simultaneously apply to every occasion that presents a challenge or requires redemptive recovery.

For an example, take the case of Sarah S., a former patient of mine. She was a cheerful and devoted girlfriend to a medical student whom I also knew well. He (the medical student) was the lucky beneficiary of Sarah's thoughtful and supportive loyalty. Partly due to her being consumed by her determination to be there for him at all costs, Sarah began to neglect her own personal self-care and nutritional needs. Consequently, she gained weight and became very corpulent. In the end, he jilted her, justifying his behavior because of her weight gain. Through redemptive AIMing, Sarah made it a goal to lose weight and triumph over her disappointment.

She did not change the world. She did not have to. She achieved her goal of shedding eighty pounds and later, to help others in similar situations, she published a well-received article about her experience. In addition, Sarah exhibited an agapeic forgiveness by attending the former boyfriend's wedding to another woman, with a message of congratulations to both, including a gift from her to the wedding couple. Throughout the challenge, Sarah said she regularly and routinely affirmed her resolve by repeatedly counting her blessings at every stage of her experience. She accepted what happened to her and eventually moved on with her life. The use of courageous surrender, of course, did not apply in Sarah's situation. She was not dying.

None of these steps in the Z Pathway are effortless, but they are commonly used every day by people like you and me who, because of a personal tragedy, have a need to reach for hope. The intensification of our inborn hungers is the ultimate impact of any tragedy; the Z Pathway, in essence, is an intensified way of reaching for hope through prayers, counting of one's blessings, forgiveness, AIMing, and finally, acceptance—with or without TCDS. Each of these steps is important for restoring peace to life after a tragedy as well as for securing the comfort of hope in the event of an impending death. With the right approach, a tragedy may and could propel you to a happier or much richer life.

Losing Theresa: My Personal Encounter with Grief

Several years ago, I had the unforgettable and most unfortunate personal experience with grief when I lost my sister, Theresa, to breast cancer. We were sharing a one-bedroom apartment in Virginia as she struggled with invasive breast cancer before, during and after radiation therapy, mastectomy, and chemotherapy. During those precious nine months spent with her, we became even closer than ever.

Few brothers could ever possibly love a sister like I loved Theresa. Consequently, her terminal illness of breast cancer was particularly difficult for me to accept and bear. We were always close and
trustful of each other since childhood. She was my older sister, and
I valued her love and devotion so much that I had often privately
prayed that I would die before her because I dreaded even imagining
a life without her.

I documented and kept a log of her fears and the acts of courage
she displayed under the weight of her illness. With her permission
I began to keep a journal as part of my human hope research, even
after I became convinced from reading the biopsy reports that she
would die of cancer. Whenever I made an entry into my journal
book about her behaviors or her answers to my probing questions, I
could not help but feel like a traitor who had chosen science over my
undivided attention to a sister I purportedly dearly loved.

When she eventually succumbed to her illness despite her many
hours of daily Rosary, I became bitter, having been a true eyewit-
ness to her unanswered prayers. Her death, though not totally un-
expected, depressed and confused me severely. My own faith in God
was seriously shaken, and life for me almost lost its meaning. I began
to question the logic of God who abandoned a woman of so much
faith and palpable trust in divine supremacy. Quite reasonably, I became agnostic and spiritually confused—a state of mind that I later
resolved using the Z Pathway.

Even as I was upset with God, I reluctantly prayed. While I was
no longer convinced about the benefits of prayers, I remembered
how devotedly Theresa prayed. I counted my blessings and was
grateful, especially, for the last months we'd spent together. It was
difficult to forgive the American embassy in Nigeria for the repeated

denial of granting a visa while the cancer got worse histologically. I even thought about suing the embassy and the U.S. State Department. Eventually, I realized that my anger was self-destructive. For my redemptive AIMing, I decided to make it a mission to adopt Theresa's youngest daughter, Judith—practically, emotionally, and financially. She became the daughter that I did not have biologically—an act that has brought so much enjoyment to my life. Judith looked so much like Theresa when we were younger. Along with being a niece and then a daughter, she became a confidant—as Theresa was. Gradually, I have come to realize that death is not a divine abandonment, neglect, betrayal, or godly inattention.

Now, whenever I think of Theresa, I smile instead of cry—having successfully completed my Z Pathway.

HAPPINESS COACHING: THE TRIPLE-H METHOD

Happiness coaching is both an art and a science. However, because there are no existing standards or prerequisites, many coaches who have inadequate knowledge of the science of happiness go into happiness coaching relying mostly on intuition and personal life experience. This chapter, "Happiness Coaching: The Triple-H Method," was written particularly to assist coaches who fall into this category. These may include life coaches, happiness officers, student counselors, directors of human resources, and others who are passionate advocates for a flourishing human community, want to become happiness coaches, but lack the knowledge of what to do—beyond their own intuitions and personal life experiences.

Theory and Practice

The theoretical basis of "Happiness Coaching: The Triple-H Method," is the Triple-H Equation: $\frac{H_1}{H_2} = H_3$ or $\frac{HOPE}{HUNGER} = HAPPINESS$. This equation, as first presented in Chapter 5 and later explained in Chapters 10 and 11, postulates that for an individual to be happy, he or she must be more hopeful than hungry. In other words, he or she must have a PHI of greater than 1.0 or the ratio of HOPE to HUNGER must be in favor of HOPE—since hope generates positive emotions and hunger generates negative emotions.

The central concept in happiness coaching—the Triple-H Method—is that if a client is effectively coached to have the appropriate mindset and also take the necessary actions that lead to an increase in hope and a decrease in hungers, the triggering of happiness will result in that client.

In practice, the entire coach-client interaction in "Happiness Coaching: The Triple-H Method" can be divided into seven stages or phases:

      Stage 1. The Initial Encounter and Intake

      Stage 2. Assisted Self-Discoveries

      Stage 3. SORKS Analysis

      Stage 4. PDR Design and Actualization

      Stage 5. Retest and Progress Evaluation

      Stage 6. The Z Pathway

      Stage 7. Celebration and Exit Interview

One by one, let's discuss these stages in detail:

Stage 1: The Initial Encounter and Intake

Happiness coaching officially begins with an initial encounter between the coach and the client at a prearranged time and place (in person or virtually). The issues that necessitated the encounter are explored. The client is encouraged to share his or her life story—as much as he or she wants to do. Socratic and very open-ended questions are asked, and answers are followed by "tell me more." From the answers during the intake process, the personal prose of a client becomes evident for appropriate *mirroring* by the coach. The learning style of the client—auditory, visual, or tactile—is unveiled and noted. Trust, empathy, empowerment, and understanding are conveyed by the coach. The role of the coach, experience, training, and certification are shared with the client. An agreement or a contract may be established and signed by both. The overall plans and goals are jointly affirmed based on the vision of the client. Personal responsibility and cooperation are emphasized. The seven stages of happiness coaching—the Triple-H Method—are reviewed and negotiated, and the necessity of personal accountability is stressed. Confidentiality, trust, and the safety of the coaching sessions are conveyed with candor and understanding. Homework assignments for the client may include thinking and presenting at the next session what possible roadblocks (or concerns) there are that could work against the vision and goals agreed upon so far between the coach and client. The purpose of the next session is explained and what was achieved at the current stage or session is enumerated, acknowledged, savored, and celebrated. The Edo Questionnaire (or PISA Scale) is given to the client for completion as homework.

Stage 2: Assisted Self-Discoveries

This is the phase of self-discoveries and self-revelations. The PISA Scale (personal instant self-assessment scale) is scored. The PHI and the zone of the client on the happiness map is determined, reviewed, validated, explained, and discussed in positive terms. The empowering nature and intent of self-discovery and self-revelations are emphasized and made known to the client. The difference between being more hopeful than hungry compared to being hungrier than hopeful is explored with the client in such a way as to elicit his or her insight about the significance of the difference. The desirability of Zone A is made clear to the client for his or her full comprehension and interpretation. The answers to the Edo Questionnaire are reviewed with the client to ascertain the reasons why they chose those answers.

The client is encouraged to make suggestions of things to be done to get a higher score. For example, looking at the client's response to statement 3 on the PISA scale: "In case of an emergency, I have someone I can count on." If the client did not circle 8 as his or her response, ask "Why?" as in why don't you have a family member, a friend, a neighbor, or a colleague you can count on in case of an emergency? What do you have to do to turn that situation around? Is it a matter of reconciliation—an apology, forgiveness, or an extended hand of sincere friendship to an estranged spouse, an alienated parent, disgruntled children, a resentful sibling, an embittered colleague, or a disaffected neighbor? Encourage the client to recognize that human family support remains a major component of a life of hope and that the best-known method for boosting human family assets is to acknowledge and respect other people's inborn hungers.

The key is to make efforts to be pleasant, helpful, considerate, and more tolerant of others. Ask the client to suggest ways he or she can widen his or her circle of friends and expand the existing pool of well-wishers. Impress upon the client to realize that if he or she does or says something nice to one different person each day for just one week, the client could have seven people with reasons to be his or her well-wishers.

Also, look at statement 5. Is the client's sub-score less than 8? If yes, why is it not 8? Why is it not "very true" that you are more fortunate than many others? If it is due fundamentally to unemployment or underemployment, then make that issue one of the client's priority goals of immediate pursuit. Help the client to realize that counting one's blessings is important and there is always something to be thankful for no matter how destitute one is. Encourage the client to be a good steward of what he or she already has, stay informed, and—if a believer—encourage them to pray often.

Next, consider every statement where the client score is less than 8. In each case, the important questions are—what exactly is lacking, and what will it take to fix it? In the case of statement 2 for example, a score of less than 7 calls specifically for creative AIMing to unveil what the client is naturally best at and consequently—boost intrinsic assets—making the client more likely to be appreciated by others.

In a similar way, analyze the client's response to statements 7–12 on the PISA Scale and help find why the response given is less than a perfect score of 1 or 2. Ultimately, the client is coached to realize that as the hope score is boosted, the hunger score automatically decreases—since a rise in *hope* lessens the intensity of *hunger*.

If necessary, homework may be assigned to the client for completion prior to the next session. For example, the client can be asked to make an exhaustive list of his or her dream vocations and passionate avocations (with instructions on how to adopt a consummate mission).

Stage 3: SORKS Analysis

In stage 3 session(s), SORKS analysis is performed. During S.O.R.K.S. analysis, the right questions are asked to elicit the client's

Self-awareness about his or her central role in the triggering of his or her own happiness. Also evoked are the client's insight into the relevance of *Others*; the right attitude about *Resources*; the power of *Knowledge*; and the importance of *Spirituality*.

For example, about **Self**... Ask—Who are you and what is unique about you? What is your greatest passion? What would you love to be known for? Are you satisfied with yourself? Why or why not? What is your calling? Do you need creative AIMing or redemptive AIMing? What specific things can you do to affirm, consolidate, and make your calling consummate and enjoyable? And just that easily, a list of specific actions that are necessary to take is generated.

About **Others**... Ask—How relevant are you in the lives of those around you? How caring, how concerned, and how considerate are you of others? How consequential would you want to be in the lives of those around you? What specific things can you do to make yourself more relevant in your community? A list of specific actions is generated.

About **Resources**... Ask—How materially sufficient are yours? What more do you wish for? How good a steward are you of all that you currently have? How blessed and lucky do you feel when you compare yourself to others in the global community? How appreciative are you of what you currently have? What specific things can you do to enhance your feeling of material adequacy and resource sufficiency? A list of specific actions is generated.

About **Knowledge**... Ask—How curious are you? What are you curious about? How knowledge hungry are you? What answers and information are you specifically looking for and unable to get? What do you know that is bothering you? How can you find out what you don't know? What specific things can you do to continuously increase your knowledge and awareness? A list of specific actions is generated.

About **Spirituality** . . . Ask—What do you think is your purpose here on Earth? How do you want to be forever remembered? What role do you most enjoy playing? What is your personal notion of God and man, good and evil spirits, or any cosmic force or forces that can influence human fate? What do you think is your mission or life mission? What specific things can you do to nurture your spirituality? A list of specific actions that are necessary is generated.

When SORKS analysis is successfully completed, the client gets good insights (and the right attitudes) about Self, Others, Resources, Knowledge, and Spirituality. This is done by the coach asking the right questions and aiding the client to arrive at the right conclusions. Happiness is about having the *right thoughts* and taking the *right actions*. The former is achieved during SORKS analysis and the latter is the reason to design an appropriately good PDR for actualization.

During SORKS analysis the client's awareness about the *role of self* is evoked as insights are generated about the personal role in one's own happiness. By asking a series of Socratic questions, creative AIMing or redemptive AIMing, a consummate mission, a true calling, or some other passionate niche for the client will emerge. People are at their best when engaged in the pursuit of their true calling and their intrinsic assets are consequently boosted.

The purpose of SORKS analysis is two-fold. The first is to help the client develop the right thoughts and attitudes. This is achieved by eliciting the right insights and helping the client to understand the roles of Self, Others, Resources, Knowledge, and Spirituality in any happy life. The second is to reveal and make apparent to the client what specific actions are necessary for boosting his or her essential human assets. Specific actions that are applicable to the client are therefore identified and included in the PDR for actualization.

Stage 4: PDR Design and Actualization

Stage 4 commences after SORKS analyses are completed. During this stage, the SORKS-inspired PDR is designed, explained, agreed upon, and offered for actualization with instructions. *PDR, personal daily routine*, is a customized and individualized set of actions or exercises aimed to *boost* the five essential human assets as well as *mitigate* the five inborn hungers, so that positive emotions are regularly triggered every day. As explained above, happiness is about having the right *thoughts* and taking the right *actions*. A successful SORKS analysis makes the former possible and PDR makes the latter a reality.

As evident in the generic template below, the PDR gives the client something specific to do every day:

Personal Daily Routine (PDR)

1. Do *something*—no matter how small—to advance your life purpose, calling, or chosen mission.
2. Do *something*—no matter how small—to put a smile on somebody's face.
3. Do *something*—no matter how small—to acquire some new knowledge, each day.
4. Do *something*—no matter how small—to acknowledge your blessings and demonstrate good stewardship over what you have.
5. Do *something*—no matter how small—to nurture your spirituality and observe your religious tenets.

The happiness coach and the client, working together, make the generic PDR become very personal, individualized, and specific for the client. They do so by finding answers to the questions: *What specific things* can the client do to advance his or her calling? *What specific things* can the client do to put a smile on somebody's face? *What specific things* can the client do to acquire new knowledge and skills? *What specific things* can the client do to demonstrate a sense of material sufficiency and good stewardship? And *what specific things* can the client do to improve his or her relationship with God, Allah, Yahweh, or any other omnipotent cosmic force of significance?

If SORKS analysis was done correctly, the answers to these questions are to be found in the *list of specific actions* gathered during SORKS analysis. The PDR is designed and perfected to answer the intrinsic assets need, human family assets need, the economic assets need, the educational assets need, and the spiritual assets need that are peculiar to the client. Possible obstacles that could prevent successful implementation of the PDR are shared, reviewed, and discussed. A mutually acceptable interval or length of time (six to eight weeks) of no sessions is agreed upon during which the PDR is used by the client as a *daily routine* and actualized.

The PDR for a student, an employed adult, the unemployed adult, or a retired senior citizen are different in complexity and specifics. Every PDR is customized to fit the individual needs and existing circumstances that were unveiled during SORKS analysis.

Stage 5: Retest and Progress Evaluation

Upon the client's return, after six to eight weeks of PDR actualization, post-testing is done, and PHI is recalculated. If progress has been made during the interval (as confirmed by actualized PDR and improved PHI), the success is acknowledged and celebrated. If there is no change in PHI, PDR readjustment is considered and the client's exact adherence to the PDR is emphasized.

Stage 6: The Z Pathway

If the client's PDR actualization, adherence, and progress are satisfactory, the Z Pathway is introduced to the client for the purpose of coping should any incidental tragedy occur. After that, an *exit interview* is planned at the discretion of the client with the support and cooperation of the coach. For the progress made to be sustained, the PDR must seamlessly become woven into the daily activities of the client—as part of everyday real life. Otherwise, all necessary adjustments and follow-ups should continue.

Stage 7: Celebration and Exit Interview

In stage 7, the original issues, requested assistance, vision, and goals are reviewed and reconciled with the outcome. When the mission is deemed accomplished by both the client and the coach, celebratory and congratulatory sentiments are exchanged followed by the exit interview. However, the relationship between a happiness coach and the client never ends. Ideally, it should blossom into a mutually rewarding ongoing platonic friendship. The necessity for further coaching sessions is left open indefinitely.

Structure: Stages, Phases, and Sessions

Although there are seven stages or phases in the Triple-H Method of coaching, each stage or phase may require multiple sessions. The complexity of the issues, the amount of assistance needed, and the unique characteristics of each client determine the pace as well as the number of sessions in each stage or phase.

In summary, the overall intent of the seven stages of happiness coaching is to identify the dreams and aspirations of the client; assist in developing the *plans* for achieving them; and encourage and motivate the client to take the necessary *actions*. Happiness coaching has a structure, and a coach must know what to do and when and how to do it. In other words, a happiness coach must have good knowledge of the art and the science of happiness coaching.

How Good a Happiness Coach Was I?

At this point, I want to share with you a happy story that I am often tempted to claim as a major success story of my happiness coaching career. It is about AJ, a forty-three-year-old female who was the assistant principal in a middle school. She attended one of my presentations and subsequently asked privately for my one-on-one happiness coaching services. During our one-on-one happiness coaching, at stage 2, her PHI was calculated to be 0.932, which is in the "unhappy" zone. At stage 4 of our happiness coaching sessions, SORKS analysis having been completed, a customized PDR that was unique to her circumstances was designed and given to her for actualization.

AJ was to return after six weeks of performing and actualizing her PDR. Instead, she showed up after three months with copious apologies for her tardiness. At post-testing, she had a PHI of 2.314—a very impressive progress. In fact, she moved from "unhappy" Zone C straight to "very happy" Zone A—bypassing Zone B. This was unusual progress but much welcome. As I was quietly starting to marvel about what an effective happiness coach I had become, AJ smiled broadly and said she had some good news to share: "I have been promoted to the rank of a full principal and, guess what? I also have a wedding engagement" as she flashed a diamond ring on her finger.

At that moment, I realized why she had taken three months instead of six weeks to return for stage 5 of our client-coach relationship. I also realized that her impressive rise in PHI may have very
little to do with my coaching efficacy. I was, however, truly happy for
her, but naturally, I became a little humbled and considerably less
self-congratulatory.

As the happiness coach who worked with AJ one-on-one, I have
been tempted occasionally to claim her *happy* story as *my* success
story. Looking at her pre-test score in Zone C and post-test score in
Zone A—as shown on the graph below—I feel very good and somewhat consequential. However, the question that still remains unanswered is: *How Good a Happiness Coach was I truly to AJ?*

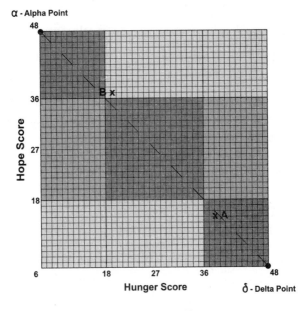

AJ Happiness Index Map

About Coaching in General

The coaching business is a fast-growing industry. In the 2020 global coaching study by the International Coaching Federation (ICF), there were 77,000 coach practitioners in 2019—an increase of 33 percent since the last estimate calculated in 2015. Also, the estimated global revenue in 2020 was 2,849 billion USD with an increase of 21 percent over the 2015 estimate. Among these coaches are life coaches, success goal coaches, physical fitness coaches, business coaches, happiness coaches, and so on. In general, happiness coaching and life coaching are very similar in many ways but quite different in certain ways. According to ICF, the main objectives of a life coach are:

1. To discover what the client wants
2. To encourage the client on the path of self-discovery
3. To inspire client-generated solutions
4. To become an accountable partner for the client

"In most cases, the clients know what they want to achieve and may even know how to achieve their goals. They do not hire a life coach in order to be told what to do or how to do it. They are looking for a support system and accountability partner," says the CEO of ICF—Magdalena Nowicka Mook. In happiness coaching, by contrast, the client wants a happier life *but does not know how* to get it. The happiness coach *understands* what blocks the client from getting a happier life and (s)he shares the right tools and strategies with the client. There is more of a "hands-on" approach in happiness coaching than in life coaching.

Interestingly, neither a life coach nor a happiness coach needs to be licensed or have any certification to start a coaching practice. Coaching is an unregulated industry and, technically, anyone can claim to be a coach. The ICF certifies Life Coach Training Institutes and has ethical standards (or guidelines) that its member institutes follow. However, individual coaches do not have to be certified and/or licensed. There are no certifying and licensing bodies for coaches.

Though formal certification is not required to become a coach, many coaches attend one of the many life coach training institutes (or programs) to be regarded (or thought of) as a "certified professional coach" by clients who are shopping around for high quality coaches.

What and Who Is a Happiness Coach?

A happiness coach is a *trained coach* knowledgeable about the art and science of helping others find a happier life. A happiness coach is different from a mentor, a teacher, or a therapist. A mentor is usually an older and wiser person from whom you can learn the facts of life; your happiness coach can be much younger than you. A teacher is a more knowledgeable person who can help you gain information and answers; your happiness coach can be less informed than you are in many academic areas or disciplines. A therapist is a clinician who can help you get well; your coach helps you to reach a goal that you have set for yourself.

Unlike a therapist, whose focus is mostly on the past and the present, the focus of the happiness coach is on the present and the future. A happiness coach is very hands on, and happiness coaching sessions can take place anywhere—at the gym, in an office, the client's home, in the classroom, or virtually via Zoom. They can be one-on-one or group sessions. A happiness coach is action oriented. He or she helps the client affirm goals; create an action plan for achieving the goals; supports and guides the client; provides motivation, and most importantly; holds the client accountable for the set goals and the agreed-upon plan of actions.

Who Needs a Happiness Coach?

1. If you are feeling overwhelmed by the everyday challenges of life—you need a happiness coach.
2. If you are an individual who, despite numerous accomplishments and apparent success, lacks a sense of personal fulfillment—you need a happiness coach.
3. If you are yearning for a fresh start or a more meaningful life; and in need of structure and professional guidance—you need a happiness coach.

When we are sick, we go to the doctor. If we have been wronged, we get an attorney. When our hair gets too long and we want to look better, we go to the barber shop or beauty parlor. Regrettably, when we are unhappy, there is nowhere to go for help, and no professional assistance is available until and unless clinical signs of depression have set in, or the risk of suicide has apparently escalated. At that stage, it could already be too late. While we all can have episodes of feeling blue, chronic unhappiness (serious, unending unhappiness of six weeks or longer) is a flashing red light and an early warning that all is not well. It is unhealthy to ignore prolonged unhappiness because preceding many cases of suicide, substance abuse, and even homicide, is unhappiness—in one form or another—that was unattended.

We need a new way of thinking about and dealing with unhappiness that lasts longer than six weeks. And it is time for a new paradigm in which *happiness coaching* is a routinely available service in the workplace, on university campuses, and in the community at large.

OVERVIEW
AND SUMMARY

The original title of this book was *The Mathematics of Happiness*, but it was later changed to *The Happiness Formula* because I thought some people might be instantly turned off due to a probable aversion to mathematics. It is, indeed, true that there are many people who think that mathematics is exclusively about numbers and quantifications—whereas mathematics is simply the *study of relationships.*

When the relationship is between numbers, as in $\frac{8}{2} = 4$, 10 x 3 = 30, or 5 + 7=12, we call that *arithmetic.* If the relationship is about shapes, space, and structures, we call that *geometry.* When the relationship is about angles, planes, and triangles, we call it *trigonometry.* True mathematicians spend a lot of time studying relationships—always looking for patterns and regularities that could provide insights that they might use to make predictions about nature—with reproducible accuracy.

Such a study of relationships is in fact exactly what I've done during my thirty to thirty-five years of research, studying the relationship between *hope, hunger,* and *happiness* that eventually led me to the discovery of the *Triple-H Equation*—and hence the rationale behind the original title of *Mathematics of Happiness.*

For many centuries, scholars from various academic disciplines— including thought leaders of different persuasions—have participated in the debates on the perennial subject matter of *hope and happiness*—wondering what they are, what they mean, how to get either or both, or how to retain, boost, or measure them.

Contrary to the notion of some psychologists, the subject matters of hope and happiness do not belong exclusively to the academic domain of psychology. We all, either as happiness seekers or happiness advocates, are stakeholders in the issue of happiness. Economists, sociologists, philosophers, theologians, poets, physicians, and mathematicians have written extensively and spoken passionately about human hope or happiness since the dawn of human civilization.

For example, one of the most thought-provoking statements that I have ever read about *human happiness* is the one attributed to the seventeenth century French mathematician and physicist, Blaise Pascal, who wrote:

All men seek happiness. This is without exception. Whatever different means they employ, they all tend to this end. The cause of some going to war, and of others avoiding it, is the same desire in both, attended with different views. They will never take the least step but to this object. This is the motive of every action of every man, even of those who hang themselves.

In this statement, Pascal, a *mathematician,* spoke commandingly about happiness as if sharing an evidence-based conclusion in quantum physics to a room full of intellectual peers. Happiness, he proclaimed, is sought after by all of us. It is the singular motive behind every human act or action, he added. It is the reason for war, the rationale for peace, and the motive of those who take their own lives. Pope Francis, a *theologian*, in an interview published in *Viva*, an Argentine weekly, gave his ten tips about *the papal recipe for happiness.* In the mid '70s, Richard Easterling, an *economist* wrote about the paradoxical relationship between happiness and national economy. Carol Graham, the research director of Global Economy and Development has written about the *paradox* of "happy peasants and miserable millionaires." Aristotle, a 300 BC Greek *philosopher*, wrote that "happiness is the meaning and the purpose of life." Also, Mohammad Gawdat, an Egyptian *entrepreneur*, and former chief business officer at Google X writes and speaks about his "6, 7, 5 Model of Happiness." Martin Seligman, a *psychologist* wrote about "Authentic Happiness." Ruut Veenhoven, a *sociologist* has written about social conditions and human happiness. Joseph Addison, the seventeenth century English *poet* wrote about the three grand essentials to happiness. Thus, as many different academic disciplines as there are, so there are different opinions and impressions of happiness, a happy life, or subjective well-being.

In addition to these interdisciplinary and different scholarly notions about happiness and well-being, the human community at large has no shortage of experiential sentiments about that thing that makes life worth living—heavily influenced by cultural upbringing, ethnicity, geography, and social class—including unique individual characteristics due to genetic predispositions. As a result, *subjective well-being* or living *a happy life* mean different things to different people. These facts have made it difficult to find *one* universal tool for measuring happiness or subjective well-being—without cultural and ethnocentric biases.

During global well-being surveys therefore, researchers have no choice but accept the different definitions of well-being harbored by the individual respondents being interviewed across the globe. The lack of a valid universal tool for measuring happiness or subjective well-being has made it impossible to *convincingly* declare any country as the happiest nation in the world or crown any one person as the happiest living human.

Fortunately, the Triple-H Equation, which says that $\frac{HOPE}{HUNGER} = HAPPINESS$ has provided us with a mathematical definition of happiness that turns out to be universally applicable to all of us—regardless of our cultural and socioeconomic differences. This equation makes it possible to assign a numerical happiness score to any human adult after he or she responds to twelve simple statements—on the Edo Questionnaire (or PISA Scale).

When fully deconstructed—as shown in Chapter 10—the Triple-H Equation helps to connect many dots in positive psychology literature, and it provides a very valid summary of the human happiness narrative. In other words, it gives the *Big Picture*.

For an analogy, imagine seven explorers, who have never seen an elephant and do not even know what an "elephant" is, had their curiosity rewarded but only under one condition. They are to be led to the zoo, blindfolded, and allowed to palpate only one specific part of a well-tamed and friendly elephant at the zoo—and then asked to give their *concluding* impressions of an elephant.

Among the concluding impressions verbalized were "An elephant is just like a rope"; "No, an elephant is like a wall"; "Oh no, an elephant is like the trunk of a tree"; respectively, from the blindfolded explorer who palpated the tail, the blindfolded explorer who palpated the side, and the blindfolded explorer who palpated the foot of the same elephant. Though an elephant has parts that fit those descriptions and impressions articulated by the three blindfolded explorers, their conclusions will certainly baffle those who have never seen an elephant or a picture of one. A lot of imagination is therefore required to make sense of a rope, a wall, and the trunk of a tree by anyone who has never seen an elephant but may be trying to make sense out of the reported findings by the blindfolded explorers. The fourth blindfolded explorer, after palpating the ear, concludes and reports that "an elephant is just like a very broad leaf." Although this conclusion is an accurate observation and a reasonable inference, it makes it no easy task to associate the trunk of a tree with a wall, a rope, and a broad leaf—for anyone who has never seen an elephant or the picture of one.

In this analogy, the elephant represents *subjective well-being*—a very complex psychological construct; the blindfolded explorers represent all of us (happiness seekers, happiness advocates, theologians, economists, psychologists, researchers, mathematicians, poets, and philosophers) who are privileged with small and very different pieces of the clues—a "rope," a "wall," a "tree trunk," and a "broad leaf" as we are all trying to find out what an elephant is.

From what we all learned in kindergarten, the pieces of a jigsaw puzzle are easier to successfully put together if a *reference picture* is available as a guide. For those who have before seen an elephant or have the picture of an elephant for a guide, "a rope," "a wall," "a tree trunk," and "a very broad leaf" can easily be put into their true and proper contexts. If the fifth blindfolded explorer were to report that an elephant is like a "large conical spear," those (who have the picture of an elephant) will rightly conclude that the tusk of an elephant is being described.

In this story of blindfolded explorers at the zoo, the zoo is the positive psychology arena, the elephant represents that complex construct called *subjective well-being* (or happiness) that we are all trying to learn more about, define, operationalize, and measure—but we're only privileged to see different small pieces of the puzzle. The *Triple-H Equation* is the *reference picture* or a guide to the entire happiness narrative.

In this book, the Triple-H Equation has provided us all with the "Big Picture" of an elephant, so we can finally connect all the dots and make sense of the "rope," "wall," "tree trunk," "broad leaf," and "conical spear." The equation authenticates the sentiments of theologians, poets, and philosophers about happiness; it explains Ed Diener's concept of set-points; affirms Chris Heathwood's desire theory; acknowledges Seligman's PERMA; corroborates the non-discredited part of Frederickson-Lozada positive/negative emotion ratio; and lastly, or perhaps most importantly, the Triple-H Equation gives us an easy way to measure and quantify the happiness of individuals—across cultures and national boundaries, regardless of socioeconomic strata.

The Triple-H Equation contradicts no established facts in the positive psychology literature. In fact, it corroborates many; I have often wondered why psychology for so long has ignored the role of *hope* in happiness and subjective well-being. In his 1969 book entitled *The Psychology of Hope*, Ezra Stoutland, who was at the time a professor of psychology at the University of Washington, acknowledged in the opening page with this statement:

> It is widely accepted that with hope, man acts, moves, and achieves. Without hope, he is often dull, listless, and moribund. Faced with a situation that threatens a loss of hope, he may desperately try to cling to it, to restore it, and to protect it. Yet despite this common awareness of the role hopefulness plays in determining behavior, rarely has it been introduced into the mainstream of psychology and psychiatry.

Disappointingly, Dr. Stoutland's observation has remained true even today despite the advent of *positive psychology*. Interestingly, Dr. Martin Seligman, "the father of positive psychology" (now in retirement), is at last espousing that *Homo sapiens* be renamed *Homo prospectus* because humans are more *prospective* than *wise* (Martin E. P. Seligman et al., 2016).

I only wish that Martin had expressed such sentiments twenty-five years ago. If he had, the Triple-H Equation could have been discovered much earlier than now. In fact, PERMA corroborates the five sources of human hope, and the Triple-H Equation strongly affirms PERMA.

I never deliberately set out to find a mathematical equation for quantifying happiness. On the contrary, the equation found me. Additional research is needed to further understand the relationship between hope and hunger as the trigger of happiness or unhappiness and the genesis of flourishing or languishing. It is my sincere desire that the Triple-H Equation will assist in making it possible to truly, unequivocally, convincingly, and unanimously agree on the happiest country in the world. And perhaps someday, identify and crown the happiest living human (HLH).

In summary, *The Happiness Formula* as a book has connected many dots, very well summed up the human happiness narrative, and condensed it into a simple mathematical equation that has made it possible—for the first time ever—to measure and quantify happiness and report it in a standardized unit of measure called PHI (or personal happiness index).

For full disclosure, my PHI is 2.923. I am in Zone A, very happy, but not flourishing—by definition. Like everybody else, I can certainly be happier.

To you, my dear reader, I say:

If your desire is a happy life, a fulfilling life, a life of inner peace and sustained contentment, here are the seven major suggestions that were elaborated upon, in various formats, throughout the pages of this book:

1. Take a fresh look at life through the lens of the Triple-H Equation.
2. Make a life full of hope your central goal.
3. Find your own niche by discovering your true calling.
4. Appreciate the entirety of your human family—the eight billion of them.
5. Recognize the available resources that are all around you—regardless of your life circumstances.
6. Remain curious so you can learn something new each day—no matter how small.
7. Find time to attend to your soul.

Frequently, motivational authors and speakers urge their readers or audience to aim high, as far as the stars or the moon. In contrast, I ask that you focus your attention here on Earth, the planet where you live and must function. I ask that you look deep inside yourself as well as around you, find your true calling, and reach for hope rather than aiming for some faraway celestial bodies.

Among the prerequisites that authors of such popular titles like *Easy Pathway to Success* and *How to Become a Billionaire* ask you to bring with you to the negotiating table are willpower, tenacity, and enthusiasm. Interestingly, these three attributes automatically come to you—effortlessly—once you find your true calling and have enough hope.

Whether you are a happiness seeker or a happiness advocate, or both; a chief happiness officer (or CHO), a life coach, or a counselor, I hope you found *The Happiness Formula* worthy of your time and a space on your mantelpiece.

Yours Sincerely,

Alphonsus

INDEX

ABOUT THE AUTHOR

Alphonsus Obayuwana, MD, PhD, CPC, is a physician-scientist, a happiness coach, and the founder and CEO of Triple-H Project LLC—an entity that trains and certifies happiness coaches. He is a Literary Titan Gold Award–winning author who has published several peer-reviewed articles in the national medical journals about human hope and happiness, including *The Hope Index Scale* that became widely used at the Coca-Cola Company, General Motors, the Veterans Administration, and many academic institutions inside and outside the United States. He is also the author of *The Five Sources of Human Hope* and *How to Live a Life of Hope*.

After thirty years of relentless research on human hope, he successfully derived the Triple-H Equation that is at the core of this book. Throughout his faculty tenures at Johns Hopkins School of Medicine, Eastern Virginia Medical school, Ohio University College of Osteopathic Medicine, and University of Toledo, he has taught and mentored medical students, resident physicians, nurses, and fellows in the art and science of caring and promoting happiness for themselves and their patients.

Dr. Obayuwana is also a retired major in the United States Air Force (Reserve). He is married to Ann Louis, his wife of forty-seven years. Together, they have two sons and three granddaughters. For recreation, he loves to walk, read, listen to music, and play his drum set.

You can find out more about Dr. Alphonsus Obayuwana by visiting www.triplehproject.com.